What People Are Saying

Pastor Tim Shoup writes with the heart of a pastor and with the skill that echoes the poetry of the hymns. His vigorous writing carries a love for the power of music, for the precision of language, and for people of God given into his pastoral care. He stands in solidarity and in need with people who need what these hymns deliver—the Gospel. This book's author stands in awe of the Gospel.

—JIM BENDER, PASTOR

Incorporating extensive research into the Lutheran Confessions, commentaries, historical background, and knowledge of music, Timothy J. Shoup writes with the heart of a pastor and master teacher. He uses personal illustrations from his life and ministry to help his readers. You will want to have your Bible at hand as you delve into this book; indeed, more than a devotional, I found it to be a deep dive into God's Word. Quoting the author, "My desire here is to spark thanksgiving to the Lord for the work of our authors, musicians, and translators." That desire is fulfilled in this gift to the Church.

—JANICE WENDORF, LUTHERAN WOMEN'S
MISSIONARY LEAGUE PAST PRESIDENT

We have largely gotten out of the habit that goes back to Martin Luther's time of using hymns to guide and nurture our meditation on God's Word. Shoup leads readers into that practice effectively with insightful, sensitive pondering that engages well-selected hymn texts. His meditations plumb the depths of these texts not only to inspire readers but also to cultivate their own use of the rich tradition of Christian hymns for prayer and praise.

—ROBERT KOLB, PR( )EOLOGY,
                                      AISSOURI

D1158790

For more than forty-five years, I've been sitting in pews and singing hymns. After reading *Praise and Honor*, I will never sit in a pew and sing a hymn the same way. Pastor Timothy Shoup insightfully and immediately draws you into the convicting yet comforting value of each line in the hymns. Personal conversations and events of real people place meanings of words from ancient hymns directly on the heart. Words written hundreds of years ago piece the events of today to actions of tomorrow. I'm amazed at how he takes so many life events and intertwines them with powerful lines and stanzas. Truly incredible.

Whether you have been attending church your entire life or are new to the faith, these devotions provide in-depth knowledge to apply the hymns to daily living. I have a new understanding of hymns that I've been singing for years due to the insightful commentary. Book marking and underlining while reading has provided me with a premier devotional reference for understanding and applying timeless hymns to my life.

—CLAY REISLER, DIGITAL LEARNING SPECIALIST

Rich with Scripture, illustrated with relatable stories, and undergirded with sound, pastoral theology, Timothy Shoup's hymn-inspired devotional is a treasure trove of meditative material for our time of private prayer. He lets us pause and think more deeply about the powerful, poetic words we sing but too often fail to absorb. Shoup gives us a renewed appreciation of these hymns as truth in the service of art, as he also finds the Christological center clothed in the sacramental life of the Church at worship. A book to be read, meditated upon, and reread again and again.

—DONALD ENGEBRETSON, PASTOR AND ADJUNCT PROFESSOR

In *Praise and Honor*, Pastor Shoup offers a series of meditations on hymns, both familiar and unfamiliar. In his devotions, Shoup balances a close study of a small group of hymns with deeper, longer meditations on individual verses. His devotions are inspired by the hymns, informed by the fullness of Scripture, and empowered by the grace of God in Jesus Christ.

—DAVID SCHMITT, PROFESSOR OF HOMILETICS AND LITERATURE,
CONCORDIA SEMINARY, ST. LOUIS, MISSOURI

Pastor Shoup puts his hand on our shoulder and invites us to step in and explore the rich world of our hymns. *Praise and Honor* illuminates the great lyrics and musical expression of fourteen hymns by his unique perspectives, his insights, and his gift of painting word pictures. Inspired by these meditations, my heart was stirred, awakened, and drawn into the love of our Savior, making the hymns speak God's Word to me and elicit my praise to Him. These hymn-inspired devotions enrich our worship by giving voice to a speechless heart, magnifying the great love of God's heart for us, and uniting our voices with the community of saints as we sing joyful alleluias to our King of kings and Lord of lords.

—SHARON SCHRADER, ST. PAUL LUTHERAN CHURCH
BONDUEL, WISCONSIN

Praise and Honor: Hymn-Inspired Devotions by Pastor Timothy Shoup is a treasury of meditations based on old hymns and new. Stanza-by-stanza insights into these fourteen carefully chosen hymns bring to the reader a wealth of personal reflections, both enhancing and enriching the hymn's content. Choosing one key line from each stanza provides the focus for this series of Christ-centered, theologically rich devotions. Written by a true hymn lover, Pastor Shoup's love for the sung truths of the Gospel and the Word of God contained in each hymn will bless the reader and be a deep well from which the thirsty may draw again and again and again. Thank you, Pastor Shoup!

—STEPHEN STARKE, PASTOR AND HYMNWRITER

Praise & Honor

HYMN-INSPIRED DEVOTIONS

Timothy J. Shoup

CONCORDIA PUBLISHING HOUSE • SAINT LOUIS

Concordia
Publishing House

Founded in 1869 as the publishing arm of The Lutheran
Church—Missouri Synod, Concordia Publishing House gives
all glory to God for the blessing of 150 years of opportunities
to provide resources that are faithful to the Holy Scriptures
and the Lutheran Confessions.

Published by Concordia Publishing House
3558 S. Jefferson Ave., St. Louis, MO 63118-3968
1-800-325-3040 • cph.org

1   2   3   4   5   6   7   8   9   10   28   27   26   25   24   23   22   21   20   19

Contents

Introduction

ne Sunday morning, a member of our congregation said to me, "Pastor, pick good hymns; no one ever leaves church humming the sermon!" She happens to be a retired elementary school teacher and a member of the generation that memorized hymns. Her suggestion came from a lifelong appreciation for the written word. Like other teachers of young children, she likes books, is good at language, and enjoys reading. Some people are not this way, however. My brother-in-law is visually and mechanically gifted. He is able to repair something by fabricating a broken or worn part, following the blueprint in his mind's eye. He would rather not write about it.

Sometimes, people can become discouraged or even bored during worship if they lack understanding of what they sing. Not every hymn, old or recently written, is easily understood, but many hymns are packed with meaning and compel further contemplation. Hymns—first and foremost—praise God precisely because they proclaim to us the saving work of His Son. They supplement the Scripture readings, support the sermon, comfort us, and join us with fellow worshipers.

I highly respect Church hymnody, with some pieces speaking the Gospel to God's children for over one thousand years, and I am honored and humbled to write devotionally in correlation with it. The fourteen hymns chosen for this volume can be said to mark milestones in the life of every Christian—Baptism and the Lord's Supper, Christmas and Easter, for instance. Some will be familiar to every reader, while others will be new. The hymns here, to me, are what my parishioners would call "good hymns" that inspire, inform, and encourage.

The goal of this book is for the Lord to use the devotions to deepen your faith in Him by increasing your understanding of each hymn's message. Each hymn is introduced with a short reading that foreshadows what lies in the devotions ahead and provides examples or explanations that will deepen your understanding of the hymn and its purpose. Then each devotion focuses on one stanza of the hymn, connects it to Scripture, explains the author's intent, and points to life application.

I invite you to enjoy singing and thinking about each stanza prior to reading the devotion. The melodies are wonderful. If you read music, great; if not, please find a friend to play them for you or employ your device and the web. Spend time with the melodies and have them in mind as you read the devotions. Regarding the hymn texts, turn to the hymn in your hymnal and think about the melody paired with the words. Ask questions. What is the stanza telling you to do, or is it proclaiming to you what God is doing, has done, or will do for you? Are any words or phrases foreign to you? I wrote these devotions as if preparing a sermon, by studying, learning, and writing first for myself. Perhaps consider, if you were to write the devotion, upon what you might focus—one point or several? I focused on one primary point in many devotions. In others, when addressing more than one point, I sometimes used subheadings.

Here is a preview of the assortment of hymns:

- "God's Own Child, I Gladly Say It" is a joyful and uplifting proclamation, putting us in touch with the gifts Christ has given to us in Baptism.

- "Let Us Ever Walk with Jesus" presents an outline of the way of life for those prepared to publicly confirm their faith.

- "Jesus Has Come and Brings Pleasure Eternal" delivers words of power with a robust tune proclaiming Jesus as Alpha, Omega, and our mighty Redeemer, whose strength sustains ours to resist temptation.

- "Gracious Savior, Grant Your Blessing" takes a full stride into the vacuum of Christ-centered wedding hymns and songs.

- "Rock of Ages, Cleft for Me," a plea for mercy, is a fitting accompaniment for your time of confession.

- "Let All Mortal Flesh Keep Silence" is hauntingly beautiful, originates from the fifth century, and draws us into the mystery of the sacrament of Christ's body and blood.

- "O Christ, Who Shared Our Mortal Life," with its rich tune, is a brilliant example of Bible storytelling and of painting word pictures. The picture is clear. Christ conquers death. And the hymn is a prayer; we ask Him to defeat death for us and to raise us too.

- Then follow four hymns appointed for Christ's life events, which mark our days as well. "O Come, O Come, Emmanuel," the cherished Advent hymn based upon seven prayers from the eighth century, calls out to the Lord to return. A new, profound little Christmas hymn, "Where Shepherds Lately Knelt," has a carefully composed, clever melody. The Lenten hymn draws from the words of Isaiah, "Stricken, Smitten, and Afflicted." A new Easter hymn trumpeting 1 Corinthians 15 is assisted by a dynamic melody that quickly became a favorite of my congregation, "If Christ Had Not Been Raised from Death."

- A friend in Slovakia with joyful determination to live for our Lord moved me to associate a hymn with the blessing of a friend who impacts one's faith. "Give Ear, O Zion, to God's Call" has a strong, familiar melody, abundant Gospel promises, and a call to live for Christ.

- When swallowed by anxiety or grief, Psalm 23, "The Lord's My Shepherd, I'll Not Want," with its sweet melody, brings peace that passes understanding from the Good Shepherd. He really did lay down His life for us and take it up again.

- Finishing with "We Praise You and Acknowledge You, O God," the hymnic translation of the ancient, majestic hymn of praise, the Te Deum, seems fitting. Ancient—we know of its liturgical use in the sixth century. Majestic—with the elaboration of all who join in praising the King of all glory, including heaven's angels, cherubim, seraphim, apostles, prophets, martyrs, and the Holy Church throughout all the world.

A few years ago, home from college one weekend, our daughter was whistling an interesting tune. "What is that?" I inquired. "It's 941, Dad. The words are really rich; we sing it in chapel, and students like it."

The words of hymns are rich, as my daughter described, because they are full of Christ. When you leave church humming a hymn, you *are* humming a sermon. That is what they are. Good hymns are good sermons full of Christ, and stanza by stanza, good hymns bring Christ to you.

It is my pleasure to give a few brief acknowledgments. I thank the Lord for the composers and authors of the hymn tunes and texts. He has given the skill to write music and verse to only a few of His children. Similarly, many pastors and laity may be familiar with the Concordia Commentary series on books of the Bible. They are invaluable. The God-given acumen and discipline of the biblical scholars allows them to step deeply into the Word of God and to open Scripture in ways few people can. Their insights shaped many paragraphs in these devotions. Further, I fondly remember and thank the Lord for a host of college and seminary professors. I am honored to mention Dr. John Eggert and Dr. Robert Kolb, each a humble, caring genius.

I am also grateful to CPH for accepting my work, and to each person there who had a hand in completing this project. I certainly thank the Lord for Peggy, my editor, for providing so many changes and suggestions to improve the manuscript. I thank the

Lord also for Jan, Sharon, Karen, Pastor Palmer, and the people of St. Paul, Bonduel, Wisconsin, for their help and encouragement.

Also, I thank God for Nancy, my dear wife, whose genuine care for me and steady manner reflects God's grace and goodness, and for my parents, Wayne and Shirley, whose modeling during my childhood taught me to hear God's voice in the Church's hymns.

May the Lord lead us to sing, *We praise You and acknowledge You, O God, to be the Lord.*

God's Own Child, I Gladly Say It

1 God's own child, I gladly say it:
I am baptized into Christ!
He, because I could not pay it,
Gave my full redemption price.
Do I need earth's treasures many?
I have one worth more than any
That brought me salvation free
Lasting to eternity!

2 Sin, disturb my soul no longer:
I am baptized into Christ!
I have comfort even stronger:
Jesus' cleansing sacrifice.
Should a guilty conscience seize me
Since my Baptism did release me
In a dear forgiving flood,
Sprinkling me with Jesus' blood?

3 Satan, hear this proclamation:
I am baptized into Christ!
Drop your ugly accusation,
I am not so soon enticed.
Now that to the font I've traveled,
All your might has come unraveled,
And, against your tyranny,
God, my Lord, unites with me!

4 Death, you cannot end my gladness:
I am baptized into Christ!
When I die, I leave all sadness
To inherit paradise!
Though I lie in dust and ashes
Faith's assurance brightly flashes:
Baptism has the strength divine
To make life immortal mine.

5 There is nothing worth comparing
To this lifelong comfort sure!
Open-eyed my grave is staring:
Even there I'll sleep secure.
Though my flesh awaits its raising,
Still my soul continues praising:
I am baptized into Christ;
I'm a child of paradise!

LSB 594
Text: Erdmann Neumeister (1671–1756)
Translation: Robert E. Voelker, b. 1957;
© 1991 Robert E. Voelker

t is the most powerful self-description on earth: *I am baptized into Christ!* Notice in the hymn the precise placement of those five words, the theme phrase, at the end of the first four lines. It draws attention and creates a *visual* exclamation point. Of course, the meaning of the phrase is most important. The text's author uses two tenses in this statement. The *ed* ending on *baptize* speaks to a matter of fact. The action has happened. Worshipers heard water splash. Through the voice of the pastor, they witnessed God call by name a new Christian to be His own child. The word before *baptized* in this testimony is not *was* to complement the past tense of *baptized*. The hymn's author does not say "I was." He says "I am!" The action is accomplished, but the effect is ongoing. It cannot fade. It will not expire. When God is the giver, the gifts keep coming. Claiming the opening phrase "God's own child" is the privilege of all who sing "I am baptized into Christ!"

We gladly say it because of what we are baptized into—Christ—and what we are baptized out of—our inbred dead relationship with God. After death with no beating heart and no breathing lungs, no one can say, "Okay, I want to get up. I've changed my mind. I want to live longer. I want to travel more and see the grandkids." A dead man cannot wish, plan, or do. He's dead. Neither can a *spiritually* dead man will or wish his way to become *spiritually* alive in Christ.

Regarding a person's faith, reason says, "We are born on the fence, with God on one side and Satan on the other, and we need to make a decision." In the land of individual rights and choices, to learn from God's Word that we are unable to come to faith and follow Jesus by our own choosing sounds strange. However, Jesus said, "Everyone who practices sin is a slave to sin" (John 8:34). He did not say, "Whoever sins chooses unwisely" or "Whoever sins will learn to stop." Paul understood this, of course, and the lesson is reinforced in his writings. Many of us can recite Ephesians 2:8: "For it is by grace you have been saved, through faith, and this not of yourselves."

But let's look back five verses to the setup. We all "were by nature children of wrath" (Ephesians 2:3). *Nature* here means "birth." Born under God's wrath does not put us close to the fence. Paul calls people *slaves* eight times in seven verses (Romans 6:16–22). Everyone is a slave, either to God and righteousness or to sin and evil. Paul teaches what Job taught. "Who can bring a clean thing out of an unclean? There is not one" (Job 14:4). No one draws pure water from a poisoned well. Holiness does not dwell in the human heart, so holy living cannot come out of it. We are unclean. Jeremiah teaches, "The heart is deceitful above all things, and desperately sick" (17:9). "So corrupt and unsearchable is man's heart that it does not wish to appear not to trust in God." What a great quote (Chemnitz and Gerhard, 147). Even when we are moved by God's love for us to love others, our actions are stained (Isaiah 64:6). When lacking desire to love, serve, and sacrifice, we might default to cunning. If we do and say nice things only to appear good, our motives are clearly visible to God, who takes a closer look (Jeremiah 17:10).

Is it necessary for God's children, the strong of faith who read devotion books, to hear strong words regarding our lost and damned sinful condition? The answer is yes. Jeremiah, who was no devotional slouch, put it this way: "Your words were found, and I ate them, and Your words became to me a joy and the delight of my heart" (Jeremiah 15:16). Yet Jeremiah includes himself among those whose hearts are corrupt and who need mercy from above. He prayed, "Heal me, O LORD, and I shall be healed; save me, and I shall be saved" (17:14). The purpose of exposing our depraved nature is to awaken repentance and, with it, thanksgiving to our Father for baptizing us into Christ and out of death and damnation. Luther believed that a small estimation of our need for Christ is matched by a small appreciation for His sacrifice.

The words from Jesus, Paul, Job, and Jeremiah bring us back to our hymn's theme. God's own children gladly say it because we need Him to rescue us, not from the balancing act on the fence between God and Satan, but out from under the eternal weight of His wrath. The author of our hymn knows the condition of his heart and the source of his hope. We gladly sing with him: I am baptized into Christ!

The author, by the way, did not write this clever hymn only a few years ago. Paired as it is with a joyful melody, I guessed it to be the work of a pastor or poet and musician from our own lifetime. Actually, the author, Erdmann Neumeister, lived from 1671 to 1756—three centuries ago. He was a pastor in Germany who wrote more than six hundred hymns, including "Jesus Sinners Doth Receive" and "I Know My Faith Is Founded," as well as church cantatas, at least five of which his contemporary Johann Sebastian Bach set to music. How our hymnal committee discovered the hymn I do not know, but I am very thankful for such a strong addition to our hymn collection.

Singing the refrain-like theme, *I am baptized into Christ*, reveals another stylistic feature. To whom are we singing? Are we comforting ourselves with the good baptismal news? The first and last stanzas do not clarify the intended receiver of the message, but the middle three stanzas clearly do. Look at the first word of the second, third, and fourth stanzas. We are not singing to other people *about* our three enemies or *about* what Christ does to them through Baptism. Rather, the author has us talking *to* the enemies themselves, as if they are evil creatures in the room (which of course Satan is). He personifies them: "Sin," "Satan," and "Death." He has us calling them to attention, confronting them head-on, and telling them what they can no longer do.

Think for a moment about the seriousness of the battle and the relentless pursuit of our enemies against us. Who has the courage to fire back at sin or to stare down death? Who gets up into Satan's face? God's own children do. Not with nonchalance or disregard for the enemies' power—we stand up to our enemies because we are forgiven and fiercely guarded by Christ, baptized into Him, into the certainty of His death and resurrection, and with His divine strength *lasting to eternity!*

> 1 God's own child, I gladly say it:
> I am baptized into Christ!
> He, because I could not pay it,
> Gave my full redemption price.
> Do I need earth's treasures many?
> I have one worth more than any
> That brought me salvation free
> Lasting to eternity!

I Am Baptized into Christ!

Years ago, as my wife and I drove across the country to my San Jose vicarage assignment, we added a thousand miles to our trip so we could see Mount Rainier. Just outside the national park, we asked the fast-food clerk which side of the mountain offered a more spectacular view. She didn't know. Nor did she have any idea what side of the park would present the most advantageous trails for viewing the mountain's massive, sprawling glaciers. "Have you ever been in the park?"

"No."

"We drove two twelve-hour days just to see it. You must have recently moved here?"

"No, I've been here my whole life, born and raised."

Who isn't stunned by a close-up gaze at a 14,000-foot mountain, except perhaps someone who has never known a day without staring at one out her kitchen window? Looking into the face of all the baptismal gifts God gives us is also a spectacular sight, one we lifelong Christians easily take for granted. The hymn's author keeps repeating one phrase: *I am baptized into Christ!* Many people, including some Christians, do not believe God accomplishes through Baptism what Paul says he does. We believe Paul. To be baptized into Christ means that through Baptism we

- have "died with" Christ (Romans 6:8);

- have been "crucified with" Christ (Galatians 2:20);

- are "buried with" Christ (Romans 6:4; Colossians 2:12);

- are "raised up" with Christ already (Ephesians 2:6);

- are made "alive" with Christ (Ephesians 2:5);

- are "seated" with Christ in heaven (Ephesians 2:6);

- will be delivered with Christ (2 Corinthians 1:10);

- will be with Christ in paradise (1 Thessalonians 4:14, 17); and

- will be with Christ in glory (Colossians 3:4). (This list is adapted from Middendorf, *Romans 1–8*, 470.)

It is not easy to define simply what this all means: to be baptized into His death; to have died with Christ; to have been crucified, buried, raised, made alive, and seated with Christ in heaven. But look again at the list. We can certainly state what all of this *cannot* mean. All of these statements from Paul cannot mean that God is doing nothing for you through Baptism.

Baptism works like Dad buckling his two sons and a daughter into the back seat. He put them in the car. They did not strap themselves in. Rather, he took the initiative; they weren't going anywhere. He backs out of the garage, heads to town, stops at the bank, goes through the car wash, picks up groceries, and detours on the way home to see the fresh snow covering the Wisconsin pines. Everywhere Dad goes, the kids go too. Likewise, everywhere Jesus goes, God's own baptized children go too, through death, into the grave, out of the grave, into His resurrection, seated with Him in paradise and glory.

This opening stanza equates Christ's baptismal gifts with the price of full redemption, which Christ alone could and did pay. During our year in San Jose, my folks came for a visit. We took a day trip to the Monterey peninsula, home to the scenic seventeen-mile coastal drive and to the famed Pebble Beach golf course. Thirty some years ago, one could tee it up at Pebble for a mere $150. On a vicar's budget, the fee was only off by one zero. My dad and I walked out of the pro shop, onto the eighteenth green, down the fairway along the ocean to the tee box, and 518 yards back up the fairway, admiring the green grass, rocks, and ocean spray. This was close to heaven. Grinning, I said, "Dad, we should really play." He didn't hesitate. He said, "I can cover my half!" Then we laughed, and we did not play. I couldn't pay, and Dad wouldn't. He did something better. Some twenty-five years earlier, he and Mom brought me to the font, where Christ does all the paying. Harold and Trudi, my godparents, by worshiping, teaching Sunday School, explaining Bible stories to me, and living with faith active in love toward everyone taught me to cherish the truth: I am baptized into Christ.

> 2   Sin, disturb my soul no longer:
> I am baptized into Christ!
> I have comfort even stronger:
> Jesus' cleansing sacrifice.
> Should a guilty conscience seize me
> Since my Baptism did release me
> In a dear forgiving flood,
> Sprinkling me with Jesus' blood?

Sin, Disturb My Soul No Longer

To whom are we singing in this stanza? We are singing to *sin*, as if it has its own mind and will. We are commanding it, as if it can hear: "Sin, stop disturbing my soul! Stop with the guilt! I am baptized!" Sin does not listen.

Some of us cannot remember a day without a burdened conscience. We might say with David,

"My iniquities . . . are too heavy for me. . . . I am feeble and crushed; I groan because of the tumult of my heart" (Psalm 38:4, 8). Once in a while, a pastor will have an experience like this: A baptized man of God will come to the office to confess his sin and will do so not with the eloquence of David in Psalm 38, but with uncontrollable, jerky breaths and gasps, and with his hands mashing his tears over his face. He will stammer to say, "Pastor, . . . I sinned . . . badly." He is carrying unbearable guilt and is feeling crushed by the lingering circumstances of his actions. He has done so much damage. Would his marriage be restored? Could he convince his children of his love? Would they ever trust him again?

Our hymn assures us that Jesus brings forgiveness and then stays with us during the aftermath caused by our own selfishness.

God connects us to Jesus in Baptism, and Jesus stays with us even through harrowing consequences.

Others of us know we need forgiveness but are not overly familiar with guilt of the magnitude of David's or of a grown man's in the pastor's study. We have not committed gross, pronounced sins against neighbor or family. How wonderful if guilt no longer seized our consciences because we are mindful of what it means to say "I am baptized into Christ" and because we have heard the powerful words at the beginning of worship: "I forgive you all your sins in the name of the Father and of the Son and of the Holy Spirit." The concern, however, is that our unfamiliarity with guilt may be because living in an uninterrupted cultural storm of godlessness leaves us unwilling or unable to recognize our own sin. Today, big sins are championed under culture's banner of acceptance, tolerance, and pleasure, and little sins go unnoticed. Desensitization to life, death, marriage, adultery, sodomy, pornography, fornication, idolatry, gossip, and greed is like a steady morphine drip. It is numbing our hearts to the seriousness of sin and also to what is truly beautiful, lovely, and honorable. We know this, and we need to care. Cultural influences are concerning, and while many of us are rightly bothered by all the sin *out there*, a good question is this: Am I disturbed by any of the sin *in here*, in my own heart?

Albrecht Peters (1924–87), a professor from Heidelberg, Germany, wrote commentaries on Luther's Large and Small Catechisms, one titled *Baptism and Lord's Supper*. In his discussion of the relationship between baptismal water and Jesus' blood, Peters cites the last stanza of the hymn "Christ, Our Lord, to Jordan Came" (Peters, 96). Spend a moment with this composite translation of that stanza:

> The eye doth naught but water see,
> Plain men the water pouring;
> But from this blindness faith is free,
> Christ Jesus' blood adoring.
> It is for faith a flood of red,
> By Christ's own blood thus tinted,
> For all our sin and weakness shed
> Which Adam has transmitted,
> And we too have committed.

In other words, Baptism is about the blood. The good news is that through the water of Baptism, we receive the benefit of Jesus' blood. The Holy Word of God, together with the physical element of water, brings Jesus' death and resurrection to the baptized. The baptismal bath is "blessed and mixed with the blood of Christ" (95).

To what end? "As His life that was offered and resurrected . . . Christ's blood comes to us in, with, and under the earthly elements, *standing guard over us in our conscience against the accusation of the divine Law*" (emphasis added, 95). We sing a beautiful rhetorical question: *Should a guilty conscience seize me Since my Baptism did release me In a dear forgiving flood, Sprinkling me with Jesus' blood?*

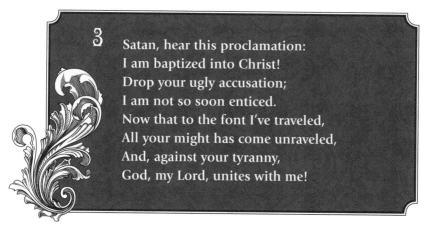

3 Satan, hear this proclamation:
I am baptized into Christ!
Drop your ugly accusation;
I am not so soon enticed.
Now that to the font I've traveled,
All your might has come unraveled,
And, against your tyranny,
God, my Lord, unites with me!

Satan, Hear This Proclamation

Steve had suffered irreversible brain damage because of cardiac arrest and septic shock. Moments after the doctor left the room, his wife, Dede, said, "Pastor, what am I going to do? I have no husband, and my son has no father." Two days later, Dede and their son, Reid, were sitting in my office to plan Steve's funeral. Reid liked "The Lamb." Dede happened upon "God's Own Child, I Gladly Say It." She asked, "Would this be good?"

I turned to Reid, "What are our three big enemies?"

"Sin, death, and Satan," he said, looking at me from under his Raiders cap.

I said to Dede, "Please look at the first word of the second stanza, the third stanza, and the fourth."

She read silently what she had heard her son say, "Sin, Satan, death," and looked at Reid with tears of hope. She had witnessed her son's knowledge of what matters.

Christ has defeated those enemies. I told her that our school-children love the hymn and that Steve is baptized into Christ. At Steve's funeral, sixty-seven children from our school filled the balcony and led the congregation in confronting sin, Satan, and death, singing, "I am baptized into Christ!" The enemies must let go.

These enemies are coming for you too. Baptism wins for us because Christ won for us.

Let's look at this a bit. Satan's accusations; an occasional stock market correction; January furnace issues in northern Wisconsin; being let go after twenty-two years—which predicament is not like the others? Life situations pinch hard. Satan's accusations damn you. We think of Satan as the tempter, given his efforts in Eden and his massive trophy case displaying remembrances of multiple wins against each of us. The hymn's author, however, knows that the immediate, hurtful consequence for each time we fall to temptation is followed by something more severe: the day of accusation. Those who grew up with landlines and manual typewriters remain amazed at how quickly one can scroll over a week's worth of texts. Smart phones store everything. When Satan scrolls back over your life, which days will he cherry-pick for your court appearance? In front of God the Judge, he will show snapshots from the favorites file he compiled against you and say, "Based on his record, allowing this miserable sinner into paradise is not justice!"

The whole matter pertains to Paul's words. "The sting of death is sin, and the power of sin is the law. But thanks be to God, who gives us the victory through our Lord Jesus Christ" (1 Corinthians 15:56–57).

"Reid, I want you to know that 'the sting of death is sin.'" I am supposed to tell him that? Isn't the sting of death, death? Sure, other men will let him drive the golf cart, teach him to hunt, or take him to ball practice, but he will never call one of them "Dad." One wonders if such a statement—the sting of death is sin—could come from an apostle, unless he never married or had children to love. Except that the statement is the Word of God. It is the Word of our heavenly Father, who Himself does know the pain of loss and death. He also knows what we cannot comprehend: Sin, with Satan's accusations against us, has the power to turn death into a trapdoor to hell.

The world refuses to believe that the moment a person meets death, something infinitely worse may yet happen. Anyone left to his or her own defense against Satan's accusations is damned.

Paul concluded the "sting of death" section with the promise: "But thanks be to God, who gives us the victory through our Lord Jesus Christ" (1 Corinthians 15:57). When Satan appears as your accuser, eager to reveal your sins, God will say to him, "You are pointing to the wrong record. Scroll over the life of My Son. He did not succumb to your temptations those forty days in the wilderness, nor on any other day. His days are made of faithfulness to Me, selfless love, service to others, suffering, and prayer—and are void of sin. And what is it that My children sing? 'I am baptized into Christ!' Yes, I have baptized them into My Son's death and resurrection, and I have baptized them into His perfect life. When you dare to accuse My children, I will point you to the record of My Son."

> 4   Death, you cannot end my gladness:
> I am baptized into Christ!
> When I die, I leave all sadness
> To inherit paradise!
> Though I lie in dust and ashes
> Faith's assurance brightly flashes:
> Baptism has the strength divine
> To make life immortal mine.

When I Die, I Leave All Sadness

Amen! When we die, we leave all sadness! This stanza expresses why, when sadness is intense and unyielding, we do not give up on life or on God and we wait for Isaiah's words to become the permanent reality:

> On this mountain the LORD of hosts will make for all peoples a feast of rich food, a feast of well-aged wine. . . . He will swallow up death forever; and . . . will wipe away tears from all faces. . . . It will be said on that day, "Behold, this is our God; we have waited for Him, that He might save us. . . . Let us be glad and rejoice in His salvation." (25:6–9)

Others may see death as a threat to the good life we are enjoying. We say we believe that the joy of paradise surpasses all, that we needn't be consumed by this world's pleasures, yet we may have difficulty living in a fashion that parallels our confession. God is delighted when His children enjoy His earthly gifts with gladness, but are we ever satisfied? A wise mother tells her bored little boy who whines and fidgets, "You don't know *what* you want!" Actually, the boy knows precisely what he wants. He just doesn't know how to get it. He wants what the sinful nature in all of us wants. He wants his definition of joy.

We know that true joy awaits us in heaven, and with Paul, we eagerly await our Savior's return (Philippians 3:20). Still, one could argue the point. We see a lot of engagement with the world: there is much racing about, picking up nice coffees and microbrews; hyperventilating over professional, collegiate, and youth sports tournaments; obsessing over social media; taking trips; building cabins; planning for early retirement; and so forth. The joy we feel because of things in this world is not automatically indicative of a selfish heart, and there is nothing wrong with wise money management, unless our love for any of this causes us to see death primarily as a threat to earthly gladness. The wonderful truth is that for those baptized into Christ, death is now the guaranteed passageway through sadness into paradise.

Can anyone describe the joy of heaven? the gladness that will be ours in paradise? This side of heaven, we cannot possibly know, but we can piece together Scripture passages that tell us what key people believed, confessed with their lives, and in some instances, died for.

Peter knows that we are sojourners here (1 Peter 2:11), and he attests, "You believe in Him and rejoice with joy that is inexpressible" precisely because you are "obtaining the outcome of your faith, the salvation of your souls" (1:8–9).

Paul is confident to say that "our citizenship is in heaven" (Philippians 3:20), that "to die is gain" (1:21), and that God will "fill you with all joy and peace in believing" (Romans 15:13).

The author of Hebrews emphasizes, "We have no lasting city, but we seek the city that is to come" (Hebrews 13:14), and John records what Jesus promised: "I will see you again, and your hearts will rejoice, and no one will take your joy from you" (John 16:22). That joy is anchored in His resurrection.

Though I Lie in Dust and Ashes

It is not problematic for the One who formed Adam from dirt to restore life to the dust and ashes we will become once in the ground. It is understandable that we do not want to leave the world because we love our spouse, children, and grandchildren. But either death cannot end my gladness or God is a liar and is using the Bible's authors to spread false hope. I cited seven passages in the above paragraph about the real joy of seeing Jesus. Here is one more where David's praise assures why death cannot end gladness:

> In Your presence there is fullness of joy; at
> Your right hand are pleasures forevermore.
> (Psalm 16:11)

5   There is nothing worth comparing
To this lifelong comfort sure!
Open-eyed my grave is staring:
Even there I'll sleep secure.
Though my flesh awaits its raising,
Still my soul continues praising:
I am baptized into Christ;
I'm a child of paradise!

My Soul Continues Praising

The first half of the second sentence makes me laugh: *Open-eyed my grave is staring*, although if I am allowed to see my death drawing near, it would not be so funny. Just as the author had us sing directly to sin, Satan, and death in stanzas 2, 3, and 4, as if sin and death are evil creatures with Satan, here he personifies the grave and paints its hunger for death.

A daughter of our congregation is a zookeeper at a small attraction. At eleven o'clock every Saturday morning, a crowd gathers there to see Rex, an eleven-foot alligator. Rex knows when it's feeding time. Sometimes Miss Zookeeper needs to go inside the fenced area, closer to Rex and his pond. Picture his beady eyes. He knows what's coming. His favorite dish is chicken, although he is not fussy. He would gladly eat the hand that feeds him. Those still eyes, staring, waiting—it sort of gives me the creeps.

If the weather is too cold, the zookeeper explained to me, gators cannot digest their food and will not eat. "I bet Rex does not like that," I jested.

"No, he doesn't. He gets crabby, and we have to be careful. Actually, though, alligators can survive up to a year without eating."

That's very interesting. And so it is with my *open-eyed grave* staring at me, always staring. It never looks away. The grave is happy to eat at eleven on a Saturday morning, or it can wait a year, or fifty, or longer. Eventually the waiting will end. The grave is going to eat.

Is it okay to laugh about the wording, about the *open-eyed grave?* It is because *I am baptized into Christ*, which means *I'm a child of paradise!* Making light of death is not denial of it or flippant mockery. It is a way of giving praise to the Lord who is resurrected, who blew the doors off of death, so to speak, on the third day. At the same time, we know death does hold the power to cripple us with the pain of loss, but only temporarily.

The open-eyed grave snapped its jaws this week in our community. A father of four, a friend to many, was found sitting in his skid steer. Members of our congregation attended his funeral at a neighboring church. His siblings, about my age, greeted the guests in the church entry—that was painful enough. His parents stood beside the casket, proud but sunken. Just inside the sanctuary, his sons stood in a row. They are young adults, similar in age to my four children. Our friend was sixty-one and healthy, we all thought. His open-eyed grave was nothing to joke about. All who mourned him felt tears, pain, reflection, repentance, prayer, but then again the great news—*Though my flesh awaits its raising, Still my soul continues praising: I am baptized into Christ; I'm a child of paradise!* It was most comforting for me to hear Paul's baptismal promises read as the pall was placed over the casket:

> Do you not know that all of us who have been
> baptized into Christ Jesus were baptized into His
> death? . . . If we have been united with Him in a
> death like His, we shall certainly be united with
> Him in a resurrection like His. (Romans 6:3, 5)

My flesh awaits its raising—a pointed testament to God's power, to our peace in Christ! We are physical beings. Heaven, the new Jerusalem coming down on the Last Day (Revelation 21:2), is physical. We have a soul and a body, and together they form one person; they are meant to be and will be together. First Corinthians 6:14; Philippians 3:21; and 1 John 3:2 are strong passages speaking to our physical resurrection in Christ. Especially encouraging to me, and I pray for you, is John 6:39. The Father has given you to His Son in Baptism. Jesus has come to do His Father's will. Jesus promises two things: He will not lose you. And on the Last Day, He will raise you.

Let Us Ever Walk with Jesus

1 Let us ever walk with Jesus,
Follow His example pure,
Through a world that would deceive us
And to sin our spirits lure.
Onward in His footsteps treading,
Pilgrims here, our home above,
Full of faith and hope and love,
Let us do the Father's bidding.
Faithful Lord, with me abide;
I shall follow where You guide.

2 Let us suffer here with Jesus
And with patience bear our cross.
Joy will follow all our sadness;
Where He is, there is no loss.
Though today we sow no laughter,
We shall reap celestial joy;
All discomforts that annoy
Shall give way to mirth hereafter.
Jesus, here I share Your woe;
Help me there Your joy to know.

3 Let us gladly die with Jesus.
Since by death He conquered death,
He will free us from destruction,
Give to us immortal breath.
Let us mortify all passion
That would lead us into sin;
And the grave that shuts us in
Shall but prove the gate to heaven.
Jesus, here with You I die,
There to live with You on high.

4 Let us also live with Jesus.
He has risen from the dead
That to life we may awaken.
Jesus, You are now our head.
We are Your own living members;
Where You live, there we shall be
In Your presence constantly,
Living there with You forever.
Jesus, let me faithful be,
Life eternal grant to me.

LSB 685
Text: Sigismund von Birken (1626–81)
Translation: © 1978 *Lutheran Book of Worship*

ach stanza's opening line ends *with Jesus*, which states the theme of this hymn and creates its familiar four-part sequence. These features emphasize the structure of our lives *with Jesus*. With Him we walk, suffer, die, and live. Stanzas 1 and 2 describe what walking and suffering with Jesus will entail. Stanza 3 explains why we gladly long to die with Jesus, and stanza 4 brings proof of why we will live with Him. In the devotion for stanza 1, we look closely at Paul's use of *walk*. With stanza 2, we contrast the perceived allure of worldly glory with the agony of *suffering*. Scripture announces that suffering is what God's children will receive and can expect, yet the Lord uses suffering to be a blessing. Stanza 3 reflects our desire to *die* with Jesus, knowing He will free us from death's destruction. In the devotion, we explore one phrase in particular: *Let us mortify all passion*. That line captures a strong component of our faith and is anything but foreign to Paul. Turning to stanza 4, we uncover a key image from the stanza's original German, which clarifies and emphasizes *living* with Jesus forever.

"Let Us Ever Walk with Jesus" is in our hymnal's "Sanctification" section. What does *sanctification* mean? The word is used to describe the work the Holy Spirit does in us to convert us to faith and to keep us in the faith, using the means God has designated: His living Word, taught, shared, or preached, together with the Word in the sacraments of Baptism and the Lord's Supper. We are familiar with Luther's explanation of the Third Article of the Apostles' Creed in his Small Catechism: that "I cannot by my own reason or strength believe in Jesus Christ, my Lord, or come to Him; but the Holy Spirit has called me by the Gospel, . . . sanctified and kept me in the truth faith." We use *sanctification* in this broad sense to include everything the Holy Spirit does to claim us, to bring us out of the clutches of Satan and into the saving arms of our Lord. Sanctification includes the Holy Spirit's action to bring to us the benefit of all of Christ's saving work. The Holy Spirit delivers to us and gives to us the benefit of what Jesus accomplished through His sinless life, crucifixion, and resurrection, not by putting a feeling in our hearts, but by creating and sustaining in our hearts a living relationship with God, that is, faith, which receives the gifts of salvation from Him.

Often, we think of *sanctification* as it relates to our daily life as God's children, the work we do and the love we offer with the Spirit and Christ dwelling in us, the baptized children of God. The hymns in the sanctification section of the hymnal pertain to Christian life, to what we do—not to earn anything from God, obviously, but in keeping with the new life that is ours in Christ. To live a sanctified life means we never give sin and temptation a free pass. Sanctification in this narrow sense means that even though we will never be perfect, we make every effort to actively live for the One who died and rose for us. We are eager to serve God in all we do, and we stubbornly resist temptation. We know the Lord's call, "If anyone would come after Me, let him deny himself and take up his cross and follow Me" (Matthew 16:24). We know that our lives in Christ are to be marked by uncompromising self-denial. We take Jesus' words seriously: "No one can serve two masters, for either he will hate the one and love the other, or he will be devoted to the one and despise the other" (Matthew 6:24). Our sinful natures feel the sting when Jesus says, "Any one of you who does not renounce all that he has cannot be My disciple" (Luke 14:33). One of our confessional documents teaches this: "Neither can there be true conversion or true contrition where the putting to death of the flesh and bearing good fruit do not follow. . . . True faith is not ungrateful to God. Neither does true faith hate God's commandments. . . . There is no inner repentance unless it also produces the outward putting to death of the flesh" (Ap XIIB 34–35).

Strong words meant to encourage us to live with commitment to Christ may also cause us to buckle with repentance. All that we do is built on the foundation of Christ's total and complete victory for us over sin and death. We are thankful for the complete and perfect self-denial Jesus lived out to cover our inability to deny ourselves, which frees us and empowers us to follow Him every day.

"Let Us Ever Walk with Jesus" has been a favorite hymn for generations. The melody builds nicely and is easy to sing.

One of the hymn's key features is the success of the author in writing a text with many phrases encouraging Christian life while simultaneously weaving in passages of comfort and assurance in Christ. It is selected for confirmations, graduations, and as one of our World War II–generation members informed me, "for our wedding hymn."

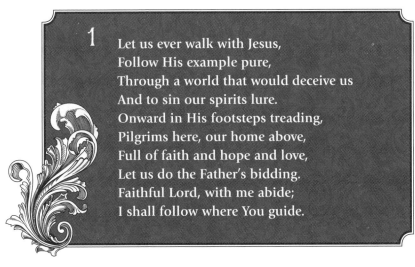

1
Let us ever walk with Jesus,
Follow His example pure,
Through a world that would deceive us
And to sin our spirits lure.
Onward in His footsteps treading,
Pilgrims here, our home above,
Full of faith and hope and love,
Let us do the Father's bidding.
Faithful Lord, with me abide;
I shall follow where You guide.

Onward in His Footsteps Treading

alk simply means "walk" when Jesus tells the paralytic what to do (Mark 2:9). Paul, on the other hand, uses the word *walk* approximately thirty times to describe and command the new life that God's baptized children live. Before proceeding with a look at Paul's use of *walk*, we will first note the important two-word opening of each stanza.

It is a soft, encouraging opening. What if the author had written *You must* rather than *Let us*? There is no command here, no ordering us about. Instead, there is a sense of gentleness, perhaps an urging, but not a shout or threat. Either way, commanded or encouraged, our old Adam is never interested in following Jesus' beautiful example; the old Adam believes Jesus' way is a restrictive pattern of rules designed to interfere with every opportunity for fun and pleasure. Furthermore, when led by the Spirit to follow Jesus, we discover the truth: It is impossible to keep up.

Yet we know that our inability to meet perfection is no excuse to quit trying. We call upon the Holy Spirit to help us resist the urging of our old Adam, because we know that God has mercy upon us when we fall behind, for it is the Lord of love in whose steps we follow. We long to walk with Jesus because we believe that His way of life—having mercy, denying self, and trusting His Father—is fulfilling, not confining. It is helpful to the people we love and even to those we do not know. Walking with Jesus gives honor to Him for having followed His Father's path through Gabbatha to Golgotha (John 19:13, 17) in order to save us.

Paul defines the walk for us because he knows that Baptism does not end our battle against Satan. Rather, it initiates it. The fight awaits us every moment. Even though the old Adam was drowned in Baptism, he still tries to be boss. He wants control. The old Adam is not merely in us; he is us. We need to be taught and told continually how to walk. Sometimes Paul's encouragement convicts us. When the sinner's shoe fits, we put it on and run with repentance to Jesus' cross. In the early chapters of Paul's letters, he convicts us of our sin and then assures us of salvation through Christ. Then, in the second half of his letters (Romans 12–16; Galatians 5–6; Ephesians 4–6; Colossians 3–4; 1 Thessalonians 5), Paul's goal is to teach and encourage us to walk in that faith. After the general manager picks the players, the coach coaches them. God has chosen us. Paul coaches us. We did not try out for a spot on His eternal roster. But now we are players, baptized into Christ, followers of Jesus, learning and trying as hard as we can.

Let's look at a few of Paul's words about walking with Jesus. Sometimes he contrasts Christlike love with promiscuity. "Walk in love, as Christ loved us and gave Himself up for us, a fragrant offering and sacrifice to God. But sexual immorality and all impurity or covetousness must not even be named among you. . . . Everyone who is sexually immoral or impure . . . has no inheritance in the kingdom of Christ and God" (Ephesians 5:2–3, 5). If Paul were the guest preacher in your church, he may say, "Ladies, present your beauty with modesty to help draw fondness, respect, and love from the hearts of men, not lust. Gentlemen, control your urges. Mothers and fathers, protect your children from internet poison. Teach your family about true love. Let them see how you love and cherish each other. Read to them His Word, and lead them to His house."

In Colossians 2:6–8, Paul associates walking with being rooted in Christ and with being taught. Listening to Jesus' Word teaches us to tune out hollow viewpoints, such as two of today's myths: "A mother's predicament is more important than her unborn baby's life" and "In the beginning was not God. No, in the beginning was matter."

In 1 Thessalonians, Paul expresses the importance of walking "in a manner worthy of God" (2:11–12). Walking worthily expresses desire to love God with all one's heart, soul, mind, and strength (Mark 12:30).

Jesus' walk took Him to Pilate and to Calvary. Walking with Jesus can be difficult because it means to struggle against the satanic foe. In full view of the cross, where Jesus won forgiveness, and with the sure hope of paradise to come, walking with Jesus is the path His followers take through a world that seeks to deceive us.

2 Let us suffer here with Jesus
And with patience bear our cross.
Joy will follow all our sadness;
Where He is, there is no loss.
Though today we sow no laughter,
We shall reap celestial joy;
All discomforts that annoy
Shall give way to mirth hereafter.
Jesus, here I share Your woe;
Help me there Your joy to know.

Let Us Suffer Here with Jesus

I admire Alexamenos! Possibly, his unbelieving classmates routinely pummeled him because God had worked faith in his heart. He was not ashamed of the Gospel (Romans 1:16). Perhaps he memorized portions of Peter's first letter and followed up his instruction to always be prepared to give a defense for the hope within (1 Peter 3:15). Were the other boys annoyed, their insecurities exposed, because Alexamenos was brave enough to keep telling them what Jesus had done? Maybe he told them that Jesus' walk on the water was nothing compared to the uphill climb He made to suffer the damnation sentence all people deserve. And maybe he told them, "He didn't only die. He rose from the dead, physically, and people saw Him."

Perhaps what sparked one boy's bitterness was watching Alexamenos pray every single day. We don't know what prompted a schoolmate to retaliate, to mock Alexamenos for his faith. However, at the Domus Gelotiana academy in Rome, on a beam, someone etched two stick figures depicting Alexamenos and Jesus. Alexamenos is worshiping, reaching upward with an outstretched arm in adoration of Jesus. It is sheer mockery, however, because the crude drawing shows Jesus on the cross with a man's body, arms, and legs *but with the head of a jackass.* In 1857, archaeologists uncovered the graffiti-like caricature and dated it to around AD 200. The mockery, the sarcasm in a caption beneath the sketch reads, *ALEXAMENOS SEBETE THEON*, "Alexamenos worships his God."

Maybe Alexamenos cherished what Paul taught the Corinthians approximately 150 years earlier: "For the word of the cross is folly to those who are perishing, but to us who are being saved it is the power of God" (1 Corinthians 1:18).

Alexamenos and our seventeenth-century hymn writer, separated by 1,500 years, are united by passages they undoubtedly both took to heart:

"Do not be surprised, brothers, that the world hates you" (1 John 3:13).

"Indeed, all who desire to live a godly life in Christ Jesus will be persecuted" (2 Timothy 3:12).

"You will be delivered up even by parents and brothers and relatives and friends, and some of you they will put to death. You will be hated by all for My name's sake" (Luke 21:16–17).

"And when they had called in the apostles, they beat them and charged them not to speak in the name of Jesus, and let them go. Then they left the presence of the council, rejoicing that they were counted worthy to suffer dishonor for the name. And every day, in the temple and from house to house, they did not cease teaching and preaching that the Christ is Jesus" (Acts 5:40–42).

"I have said these things to you, that in Me you may have peace. In the world you will have tribulation. But take heart; I have overcome the world" (John 16:33).

When suffering comes, we look to Christ's promises. We believe Peter's assurance that we have "an inheritance that is imperishable, undefiled, and unfading, kept in heaven," and in this we rejoice "though now for a little while, if necessary, you have been grieved by various trials" (1 Peter 1:4, 6). We are comforted by what matters most: "And this is the will of Him who sent Me, that I should lose nothing of all that He has given Me, but raise it up on the last day" (John 6:39).

Bo Giertz (1905–98), a gifted, faithful, twentieth-century Lutheran pastor and bishop in Sweden, teaches another purpose for suffering that comes to us through others. God could end it by wiping out everyone who sins against us. Doing so, however, would mean immediate damnation for every unbelieving evildoer. God is determined rather to use all possibilities to convert more of His lost children; He wants no one to perish. Our merciful God allowed time for you and me to be brought to Him, whether in infancy or later. And so we, too, must be willing to suffer so that forgiveness may continue to be preached to an unbelieving populace (*To Live with Christ*, 715).

And after you have suffered a little while, the God of all grace, who has called you to His eternal glory in Christ, will Himself restore, confirm, strengthen, and establish you. (1 Peter 5:10)

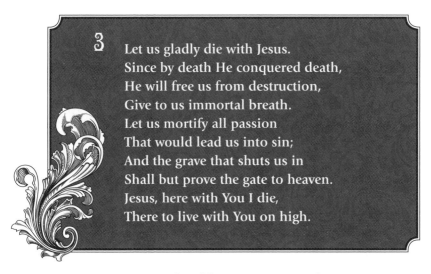

3

Let us gladly die with Jesus.
Since by death He conquered death,
He will free us from destruction,
Give to us immortal breath.
Let us mortify all passion
That would lead us into sin;
And the grave that shuts us in
Shall but prove the gate to heaven.
Jesus, here with You I die,
There to live with You on high.

Let Us Gladly Die with Jesus

This stanza reminds us that Jesus' death vanquished eternal death. Let us not fool ourselves, however. The grave will shut us in. I don't know if I could watch the gravedigger crank the handle of the winch to lower into the ground the casket holding my own daughter or son. The pain, the finality of a child torn away by death, would be unbearable—except that the separation mortal death causes is not final. Praise God, Christ turns the grave into a gateway, a safe and direct pathway to glory. Stanza 3 uses five phrases to assure us of what Jesus has done to death and of what He will do for us through it:

- He conquered death.

- He frees us from its destruction.

- He gives to us immortal breath.

- He has turned the grave into heaven's gate.

- He will bring us to be with Him on high.

One phrase, however, is the focus of this devotion: *Let us mortify all passion.*

If we let ourselves satisfy our lusts and passions, damnation looms. The hymn's author believed it. We must remember it too.

> Do not be deceived: God is not mocked, for whatever one sows, that will he also reap. For the one who sows to his own flesh will from the flesh reap corruption, but the one who sows to the Spirit will from the Spirit reap eternal life. (Galatians 6:7–8)

Some people may be tempted not to take these Bible verses seriously. Everyone needs to. Paul speaks God's truth. We must strive to kill any desire to live against God's good will. Sometimes God does the mortifying. He causes or allows struggles and deep pains to humble us, to lead us to repent, to lead us to love Him more and this world less.

If you were to list ten people with strong faith, from the Bible or from your life, Paul would be near the top. He walked repeatedly into certain death to proclaim the Gospel to those who hated God, His Son, and His apostle. He received the thirty-nine lashes on five occasions. He was beaten with rods three times (2 Corinthians 11:24–25). And he was stoned to death, or so his enemies thought. Paul recovered and kept preaching (Acts 14:19–23). He had no fear of death. He had absolutely no fear of what man could do to him (Psalm 118:6; Matthew 10:28). God worked in him unshakable faith and trust.

Paul teaches us to mortify the flesh, and he practiced what he preached. "I discipline my body and keep it under control, lest after preaching to others I myself should be disqualified" (1 Corinthians 9:27). The first half of the verse causes self-evaluation. The second half is astounding. He does not say that he disciplines his body in order to remain healthy for a long life of service, at least not in this verse. He says that he fears disqualification. Why would Paul be concerned about losing his faith? If the depth of Paul's faith is measured by his willingness, under the threat of death, to confront others about their sin and proclaim to a pagan world that the dead Christ came back to life on the third day, then his faith and fearlessness are unfamiliar to us. What John the Baptist said of Jesus, we can say of Paul: "I am not worthy to untie his sandal." However, Paul still has the sinful capacity to kill his own faith, and he knows it. The fastest way to succeed at this would be to feed his passions. Quit fighting sin, and sin moves in. Stop fighting this kind of cancer, and it will not stop. Determined as he is to live for God in all things, Paul still respects the threat to his salvation posed by his evil, sinful nature. Perhaps we should take note. Paul does not want what happened to Demas to happen to anyone else (2 Timothy 4:10). Paul exhorts us to continually resist the reign of sin in our mortal bodies so we do not wind up obeying its passions (Romans 6:12). Sin is always trying to regain control by getting us to listen to its urgings. Paul encourages us, with the strength of Christ working in us, to "be steadfast, immovable, always abounding in the work of the Lord" (1 Corinthians 15:58), and to "be watchful, stand firm in the faith, act like men, be strong" (16:13). Paul does not ask whether satisfying a desire feels good. Good feelings do not justify harmful behavior. Paul fears that feeding worldly passions will leave us contented apart from the cross and indifferent to it.

It's important to understand that mortifying the flesh does not add to the sacrifice Christ already made for us. That is not the idea, not at all. Striving to resist the sinful nature—not wanting sin and sinful desires to drive the bus of faith into the ditch of perdition—is the issue. Paul says, "Resist"; Jesus commands, "Deny yourself"; and John says, "Do not love the world or the things in the world" (1 John 2:15). Many of us are doing this as best we can every day. Others of us may need to compare, for example, the effort we give to disciplining ourselves against selfish, sinful desires with the energy we expend to make sure we are entertained. Christ has assured us victory. Triumph over sin is ours. We are baptized into Christ, buried with Him, and raised with Him. Our citizenship is in heaven. Satan is and remains defeated. Hell is not for us. Christ's tomb echoes hollow. The cross remains stained by His blood for our sin. The mysterious tension and struggle persist for us, however. Until the Lord takes us through the grave, the gateway to heaven, or until He returns, God's baptized children strive to *mortify all passion that would lead us into sin.*

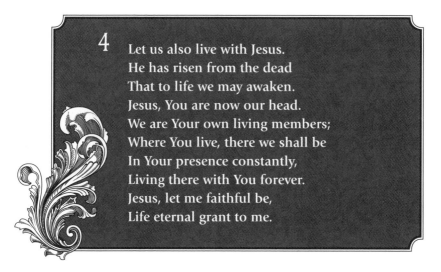

4 Let us also live with Jesus.
He has risen from the dead
That to life we may awaken.
Jesus, You are now our head.
We are Your own living members;
Where You live, there we shall be
In Your presence constantly,
Living there with You forever.
Jesus, let me faithful be,
Life eternal grant to me.

Let Us Also Live with Jesus

Walking with Jesus is not easy. The world lures us into sin, which is exactly where our human nature likes to go. The redeemed man, however—the new child of God who is baptized into Christ—hates sin, loves God, deeply desires to *follow His example pure*, and is delighted to know that we are pilgrims passing through. Our home is above because Christ came down. He loves us. He died for us and for our salvation. Then He "ascended into heaven," as we profess in the Creed, but He will return for us, and we will enjoy the new heaven and the new earth with Him. For now we are like hotel guests, away from home, renting a space where we will not remain for long. We are on our way home, looking forward to seeing family, to settling in, to being with Jesus. On our way, we try to live as Jesus did, as Paul teaches, worthy of God with care for our neighbor.

We are not surprised when suffering comes on account of our walking with Jesus and taking a stand for Him. Amazingly, after taking the beatings for speaking in Jesus' name, the apostles leave the area rejoicing that they were counted worthy to suffer for Jesus (Acts 5:40–42). Jesus did not say, "Pick some nice flowers and follow Me." Crosses are heavy and hard to carry, but Jesus has "overcome the world" (John 16:33), and He promises to restore us after we have suffered while here (1 Peter 5:10). We walk with Jesus, suffer with Him, and die with Him. Crosses bring death. That is their purpose, literally and figuratively. God uses crosses, the suffering we encounter, to mortify our passions, to drown our sinful nature through repentance day after day, and to keep our pride in check and our faith strong. Then, when the day does come for us to leave this earth, we die with Jesus, with the one who conquered death and frees us from destruction, whose grave could not shut Him in, who takes us through the tomb into life with Him.

Believers walk, suffer, and die with Jesus, and sing in full voice: *Let us also live with Jesus. He has risen from the dead.*

The guards at the tomb became like dead men at the sight of the angel who sat upon the stone he had rolled back. Then they went and told the chief priests all that had taken place. The priests and elders bribed the guards to tell the people that Jesus' "disciples came by night and stole Him away while we were asleep" (Matthew 28:2-4, 11-13). What a silly story. Would you have believed the guards? If the guards were sleeping, how did they know what the disciples did? If asleep, would they not have awoken to the big rock rumbling away? Besides that, Roman guards do not sleep and tell. We've all heard about the fate of drowsy guards, derelict of duty. Doubts, bribes, lies, and skeptics cannot change the truth. The angel said to the women, "I know that you seek Jesus who was crucified. He is not here, for He has risen, as He said" (Matthew 28:5-6). We will live with Jesus too.

If we translate the lines from the original German without concern for rhyme and meter, we have the following:

> Let us live with Jesus;
> Because He has risen,
> The grave must give us back.

Jonah's fish had to cough him up. God made the large fish, and He made the large fish listen. It spat out Jonah. "For just as Jonah was three days and three nights in the belly of the great fish, so will the Son of Man be three days and three nights in the heart of the earth" (Matthew 12:40). Jesus knew Jonah's story and His own. The fish, that's one thing. The grave, the ultimate large mouth of death, is another—but it must answer to the Lord of life, to the One who Himself came back from death.

Yes, we are the Body of Christ; He is our Head, and we are the living members, and where Christ is, there we will be. It is a beautiful threefold promise—where, with whom, and for how long:

> *Where You live, there we shall be*
> *In Your presence constantly,*
> *Living there with You forever.*

Jesus Has Come and Brings Pleasure Eternal

1 Jesus has come and brings pleasure eternal,
   Alpha, Omega, Beginning and End;
   Godhead, humanity, union supernal,
   O great Redeemer, You come as our friend!
   Heaven and earth, now proclaim this
       great wonder:
   Jesus has come and brings pleasure eternal!

2 Jesus has come! Now see bonds rent asunder!
   Fetters of death now dissolve, disappear.
   See Him burst through with a voice as
       of thunder!
   He sets us free from our guilt and our fear,
   Lifts us from shame to the place of His honor.
   Jesus has come! Hear the roll of God's thunder!

3 Jesus has come as the mighty Redeemer.
See now the threatening strong one disarmed!
Jesus breaks down all the walls of
    death's fortress,
Brings forth the pris'ners triumphant,
    unharmed.
Satan, you wicked one, own now your master!
Jesus has come! He, the mighty Redeemer!

4 Jesus has come as the King of all glory!
Heaven and earth, O declare His great pow'r,
Capturing hearts with the heavenly story;
Welcome Him now in this fast-fleeting hour!
Ponder His love! Take the crown He has
    for you!
Jesus has come! He, the King of all glory!

LSB 533
Text: Johann Ludwig Conrad Allendorf (1693–1773)
Translation: Oliver C. Rupprecht (1903–2000); © 1982 CPH

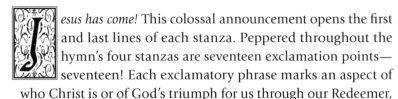

esus has come! This colossal announcement opens the first and last lines of each stanza. Peppered throughout the hymn's four stanzas are seventeen exclamation points— seventeen! Each exclamatory phrase marks an aspect of who Christ is or of God's triumph for us through our Redeemer, all stemming from one fact—*Jesus has come!*

A powerful, robust tune enhances each stanza's strong Gospel points. If you look at *Lutheran Service Book* 533, you will see that in the second line of each stanza, a note is repeated three times before we sing a steep interval to the high note on which lands a key word or syllable. In stanza 1, it is *Omega's* middle syllable; in stanza 2, *death*; in stanza 3, the first syllable of *threatening*; in stanza 4, *earth*. Two lines below, the three notes and ascending interval repeat, and again a primary word or syllable is joined to the high note of the musical phrase. This is not accidental. The translator's failure to do so would result in a clumsy mismatching of notes and words and would make the hymn difficult to sing and comprehend. For example, the words *Omega* and *Redeemer* in stanza 1 are three syllables each, with the accent on the second syllable, the very syllable that lands on the high note of the musical phrase. Imagine, however, taking the word *O* out of the phrase *O great Redeemer*. The phrase loses one syllable which causes *er*, the third syllable of *Redeemer*, to land on the high note. How awkward if we were to sing *great Re-deem-ER* instead of *O great Re-DEEM-er*.

What seems natural, having words and notes matching nicely, is necessary, not automatic. My desire here is to spark thanksgiving to the Lord for the work of our authors, musicians, and translators. The combined work of each in this hymn causes a seamless, unified sense serving the goal of every hymn—to bring the message of Christ and His saving work to His people.

Now, let's preview this text, together with how the Lord uses it for our benefit. The first stanza, using titles fitting for no one else on earth, introduces the One who has come. Consider the contrast between His title and His relationship to you expressed in the stanza. He who is Alpha and Omega, Beginning and End, fully God and fully man, comes as your friend. What is the highest status of any of your other friends? Only your friend Jesus has come to make your fetters of death, your guilt, and your fear disappear (st. 2). What is more, He has come as your friend to disarm the murdering, lying ruler of this age (st. 3). Do people in your circle ever mention Satan? Praising God with the declaration of Satan's defeat means more when we believe the seriousness of his threat. Satan is determined to destroy you. Do not doubt it. But Jesus has come to disarm this strong one. Jesus' resurrection proves that the world's prince is no match for the Lord of all. He Himself says, "I am the first and I am the last; besides Me there is no god" (Isaiah 44:6).

Heaven and earth—all of creation and all saints—declare the power of the Alpha and Omega, the King of all glory, capturing hearts with the heavenly story of Jesus' power over Satan and death (st. 4).

This hymn's triumphant tone fills our hearts with the message of who Christ is and what He has done, does, and will do for us, and thereby increases our fear of, love for, and trust in Him.

- Jesus has come.

- He disarmed Satan.

- He overpowered death.

- He took into Himself our sin.

- He sets us free from our guilt and our fear.

- He lifts us from shame to the place of His honor.

- He gives us eternal joy.

Here is an additional outcome: the hymn's proclamation empowers us to fight temptation. Hearing what Jesus does changes what we want to do. Satan keeps tempting us to care less, to lust more, to live life to the fullest, which often means "for oneself." The truth in this hymn draws us closer to Him, deepens our understanding of the riches of the eternal joy that is ours, and empowers the new man created in us through Baptism to love

God, give Him honor, resist temptation, seek what is truly good, and live for others.

Many hymns serve to build up courage and strength. And this hymn, assigned to the "Redeemer" section of hymns in *Lutheran Service Book*, could be assigned to other sections as well, such as "Epiphany," "Praise and Adoration," and "The Church Triumphant." Let us think of it also as bringing a strong word that the Lord uses to build up resistance against temptation in the hearts of His children.

> 1 Jesus has come and brings pleasure eternal,
> Alpha, Omega, Beginning and End;
> Godhead, humanity, union supernal,
> O great Redeemer, You come as our friend!
> Heaven and earth, now proclaim this
>   great wonder:
> Jesus has come and brings pleasure eternal!

Jesus Has Come and Brings Pleasure Eternal

The first three words could support five hundred sermons. Hearing these words, saying them aloud, thinking about who Jesus is, where He came from, meditating on what He did here, realizing that He comes as our friend, and we have to wonder why we are easy targets of temptation. Temptation keeps coming, for now, but the end for temptation is coming too. It is a part of our eternal joy—no more temptation, no more pain, no more sin! *Pleasure eternal* is not an additional thing that Jesus brings. Jesus is not the delivery man who drops off a package of joy. He *is* the joy. God was the joy for His Old Testament people. "Strength and joy are in His place" (1 Chronicles 16:27), the people sang after King David and the commanders of thousands brought up the ark of the covenant of the Lord, which served as the throne of God's holy presence (1 Chronicles 15:25–16:1). The psalmist knows that the gifts of grain and wine do not compare to the joy that the Lord puts in his heart when He makes His face shine upon him (Psalm 4:6–7). The worshiper rejoices when God sends the light of His truth, and he goes to the altar to praise God, his exceeding joy (Psalm 43:3–4). The psalmist and all Christians rejoice because the Lord makes known to us the path of life, there is fullness of joy in His presence, and pleasures forevermore are at His right hand (Psalm 16:11). John the Baptist leaps for joy in the womb of his mother at the hearing of Christ's blessing through Mary's greeting (Luke 1:44). Jesus' coming into the world is the great joy announced by the angel (Luke 2:10–11). And Jesus promises His disciples at the time of His departure, "You have sorrow now, but I will see you again . . . and no one will take your joy from you" (John 16:22). There is no sadness such as being without Jesus, no greater joy than being with Him. *That* is pleasure eternal.

Pleasure eternal comes with Jesus because He is the Alpha and Omega, the transcendent, everlasting presence of God beyond all creation. The Alpha and Omega is infinitely eternal, subject to nothing. Jesus, the Alpha and Omega, with the Father and the Spirit, is not a creature. He makes creatures. Jesus, the Alpha and Omega, is fully divine, "begotten, not made, being of one substance with the Father" (Nicene Creed), and fully human, completely faithful to His Father, taking the eternal punishment of our sins and bringing the eternal joy of paradise. Jesus, the Alpha and Omega, gives us reason and power to fight temptation and more. Jesus, the Beginning and the End, brings eternal joy—the end to this world, the new beginning when there will be no temptation *or* sin!

Pleasure eternal means that Jesus comes as our friend! Zacchaeus needed the one-of-a-kind friend who could lay down His life for his trespasses. Luke tells us that the only chief tax collector mentioned in the New Testament, rich and despised, climbed a tree to see Jesus (Luke 19:1–10). A rich man climbed a tree. Maybe the guilt was getting to him. Have you experienced it—guilt so sticky it saps your time and sleep and steals your sense of presence and ability to think? Zacchaeus gazed from a distance. Jesus went up to him and insisted, "Zacchaeus, hurry and come down, for I must stay at your house today" (v. 5). Jesus surprised the sinner with grace and shocked the self-righteous, money-loving Pharisees. In place of his ill-gotten gains, Zacchaeus receives Jesus' treasures, the eternal joy money cannot buy.

Feeling tempted or guilty, or guilty for not feeling guilty? No need to run or climb. Sit in devotion with the Lord, who comes to your house in His Word. Today, Jesus is with you. Today, the

Alpha and Omega, who exists beyond all creation and who came to earth, takes away your sins and gives you power over temptation. Today, the great Redeemer, who laid down His life for His friends, gives you eternal joy.

> 2   Jesus has come! Now see bonds rent asunder!
> Fetters of death now dissolve, disappear.
> See Him burst through with a voice as
>   of thunder!
> He sets us free from our guilt and
>   our fear,
> Lifts us from shame to the place of
>   His honor.
> Jesus has come! Hear the roll of
>   God's thunder!

Fetters of Death
Now Dissolve, Disappear

Fetters dissolve for some, but not for all. Read Acts 12:1–19. There we see a wave of persecution come over God's people. The fetters held James—Herod the king beheaded him. When he saw that it pleased the Jews, he seized Peter. He was bound by chains to two guards, and two sentries were posted at the prison door as additional security. As Peter awaited the sword, God's people prayed. Then, on what Herod had planned to be Peter's last night, an angel of the Lord woke Peter and urged him to move quickly. His shackles fell, the outer gate opened, and they went out to the street. The angel left, and Peter went to Mary's house, where the people were praying. Rhoda, a servant girl, recognized his voice when he knocked on the door, but in her excitement, she failed to let him in. She rushed to the others, interrupting the prayer circle inside to tell them who stood outside. "You are out of your mind," they insisted (v. 15). Peter kept knocking, and when they opened the door, they were amazed. Rhoda's words were true, and they heard Peter describe his miraculous escape.

The fetters of death dissolved for Peter—the Lord slipped the shackles from his hands.

Last week, Nancy and I returned from a trip to Washington, DC, with our eighth-grade class. One of the many things we did was visit the Vietnam Memorial to see the names of the fallen etched into the wall. Those names are not listed alphabetically; they are arranged chronologically, according to the day of death. Imagine being a Vietnam veteran, perhaps having lost four friends one afternoon, and fifty years later locating their names, all four together, and wondering, why did the fetters of death disappear for me and not for them?

The cyclorama at the Gettysburg visitor center is a cyclorama oil painting on canvas, 377 feet in circumference and 42 feet tall. The exhibit is enhanced with flashes of light and battle sounds. The magnificent display places the viewer in the center of Picket's Charge and simulates cannon, blood, and gunshot. More than a hundred and fifty years ago, real men lay busted open in hot weather, groaning for help, fearful of death, knowing that if their injuries were worse than a wounded arm or leg, they would be left to die. And die they did. During the three-day span, the fetters of death did not let go of fifty thousand soldiers.

The temptation to think that death is not fair—which is another way of saying that God is not fair—is not easy to resist when death comes to the good, the heroic, and the young. The truth is that death is not a matter of fairness. It is a matter of compensation. Compensation is earned. It is not freely given. Paul says exactly that in Romans 4:4: "Now to the one who works, his wages are not counted as a gift but as his due." He stresses the concept two chapters later with the familiar verse "The wages of sin is death" (6:23). God set the wage, Paul posts it, and everyone earns it: death, the sinner's wage. Each sinner is fully compensated. Faithful to God or unbelieving, young, old, healthy or not, the fetters of sin never let go of us. Peter escaped prison, but not the cross. Soldiers survive, but their ultimate compensation is paid eventually, and so is yours. So do the fetters of death dissolve and disappear or not?

In his commentary on Ephesians (*Ephesians*, 296 and following, especially 298–99), Professor Winger looks to the middle of Ephesians 2:1–10 to see the heart of the section. A sentence employing three powerful verbs and one key phrase allows us to hear the passion in Paul's voice:

> But God, being rich in mercy, because of the great love with which He loved us, even when we were dead in our trespasses, made us alive together with Christ—by grace you have been saved—and raised us up with Him and seated us with Him in the heavenly places in Christ Jesus. (Ephesians 2:4–6)

The key phrase is *by grace you have been saved*. Yes, of course the fetters dissolve! By grace you have been saved. Jesus has saved you from death! The verbs *made us alive, raised us up,* and *seated us with Him*—these miracles of grace given to you in Baptism—add vivid emphasis to the proclamation "you have been saved." If He has made you alive, raised you, and seated you with Him unto everlasting life, then it is certain that *the fetters of death now dissolve, disappear,* for, indeed, He *lifts us from shame to the place of His honor.*

> 3 Jesus has come as the mighty Redeemer.
> See now the threatening strong one disarmed!
> Jesus breaks down all the walls of death's
>   fortress,
> Brings forth the pris'ners triumphant,
>   unharmed.
> Satan, you wicked one, own now your master!
> Jesus has come! He, the mighty Redeemer!

See Now the Threatening Strong One Disarmed!

One concern in this devotion is not that we doubt the certainty of the stanza's second line. We know that our Redeemer has disarmed our evil foe forever. Jesus showed His power over the devil on Easter morning. The concern is that we will be tempted not to take Satan seriously even though we know that he always tempts. When possible, he terrorizes. But those who have a life-long embedded attraction to sin present little challenge to Satan. Those who resist the devil and look to Jesus for strength are the ones he threatens the most. The wicked one aims to do us bodily harm. See Luke 13:11–16 for the story of a woman Satan bound for eighteen years, or Matthew 8:31–32 for a refresher on how much he enjoys destroying and killing. The prize he seeks most is our faith. He wants to kill it. Just because many of us are familiar with Peter's warning doesn't mean we aren't in danger. The evil one is always looking for someone to devour (1 Peter 5:8) by whatever means possible.

Do you know what ingredients are in rat poison? There are two. Look on the side of the yellow box. You will see POISON—0.005% and FOOD—99.995%; TOTAL—100.00%. How much is .005%? Think of it this way: it is one half of 1/1,000 of 1%.

Dump 100 pellets out of the box of rat poison. Smash one into 1,000 pieces, and then slice one of those pieces in half. And that's it. That's the amount of poison. The poisonous trace is undetected by the hungry rodent. For many years, society pointed out what was poisonous to children's well-being, marriage, family, community, and faith. Satan had to stir into life's food chain undetectable traces of ungodliness to form his attack. Today, Satan gets away with inserting a high percentage of faith-numbing information and activity into society's diet plan, a proportion of contaminant so high that if the same quotient of poison were mixed in with rat food, no rodent would go near it.

There is fallout from this intense poisoning. The fallout is that in our country today, a smaller percentage of people are closer to God than ever before. The fallout is that Satan's impact through culture's poison keeps many unbelievers in their condemned state and weakens the faith of many believers. The fallout is that we may be less inclined to recognize our sin and therefore less grateful to our Savior. A counterattack against the temptation not to take sin and Satan seriously is to earnestly prepare for worship, for Confession and Absolution in the Divine Service. The words of the apostle John in that opening are pertinent:

> If we say we have no sin, we deceive ourselves and the truth is not in us. (1 John 1:8)
>
> Let us then confess our sins to God our Father. (*LSB*, p. 151)

When we humble ourselves in self-examination, confess, repent, and hear Him say again through the pastor's voice, "*I forgive you all your sins*," the Holy Spirit enlivens faith, increases joy, and awakes our defenses to Satan's tactics.

Jesus breaks down all the walls of death's fortress. Meanwhile, Satan remains proud of death's fortress. He loves death and the seemingly invincible walls around it. Death's fortress is impenetrable to us, but not to God. And He did not delay the attack against Satan's fortress of death. In Genesis 3:15, He promised a head-crushing blow. Generations later, when the angels sang at the Baby's birth (Luke 2:14), death's fortress and Satan's legion were served notice. When Jesus withstood physical temptation by going without food for forty days, the foundation of death's fortress shook (Luke 4:1–13). When God the Son took the hand of a dead little girl and said, "Talitha cumi" (Mark 5:41), when He touched the widow's son's bier and said to her, "Do not weep" (Luke 7:13), and when He came to the tomb of Mary and Martha's brother and said, "Take away the stone" (John 11:39), the fortress walls of death were crumbling because three dead people were living. And when the angel said to the women, "Do not be afraid, for I know that you seek Jesus who was crucified. He is not here, for He has risen" (Matthew 28:5–6), our eyes of faith see death's fortress fallen like the wall of Jericho (Joshua 6:20).

4 Jesus has come as the King of all glory!
Heaven and earth, O declare His great pow'r,
Capturing hearts with the heavenly story;
Welcome Him now in this fast-fleeting hour!
Ponder His love! Take the crown He has
for you!
Jesus has come! He, the King of all glory!

Heaven and Earth,
O Declare His Great Pow'r

One summer evening, we sat on the deck at our daughter and son-in-law's home in northwest Wisconsin, enjoying the woodsy backyard. There appeared tiny flashes of light a few feet in front of us, one here, another there—lightning bugs in the yard. Our three-year-old grandson was delighted. Then the light show switched from fireflies to high-voltage lightning bolts. Dramatic flashes, some striking down as if in attack mode and others flashing horizontally as if assigned to illumination duty, caused us to watch with anticipation for forty-five minutes until the mosquitoes drove us inside. Faint rumbles indicated that the electric charges were not as close as they seemed. *Heaven and earth, O declare His great pow'r.*

Northeastern Wisconsin has rolling hills, farm fields, and dense woods. It's a three-mile hike, with a steep hill, from our front door to our neighbor's roadside mailbox and back. This morning's 58-degree air felt warmer with a bright sun. In the first half mile, we passed orange day lilies lining the ditch, yellow goldfinches flitting their way down a row of corn, and a monarch butterfly—striking to the eye with jet-black veins against orange. The hill causes the corn, bean, and alfalfa fields to be pitched downward west to east, displaying their contrasting shades of green. A bit to the north, a patch of woods with a silhouette of towering pines is nestled behind the fields. Every day, the beautiful scenery serves as reminder. God graciously gives to us our daily bread and bountiful resources through His creation, and it does *declare His great pow'r.*

Creation gives praise to the Creator, and God's children praise God for creation. However, what truly captures our hearts and moves us to praise—and to fear, love, and trust God—is the heavenly story that you well know. The Father of all mankind sent His only Son into the broken world to save us, redeem us, pay the price of our salvation. At the heart of all incentive to praise the Creator is His endless stream of grace, granting us forgiveness and everlasting life.

Much of the story of Nehemiah involves God's care in using him to rebuild the Jerusalem wall nearly 150 years after its destruction. His task was completed in only fifty-two days. The people were moved to call upon Ezra to read Scripture (Nehemiah 8), and they wept as they heard the Law (v. 9). They planned a special worship service:

Now on the twenty-fourth day of this month the people of Israel were assembled with fasting and in sackcloth, and with earth on their heads. And the Israelites separated themselves from all foreigners and stood and confessed their sins and the iniquities of their fathers. And they stood up in their place and read from the Book of the Law of the LORD their God for a quarter of the day; for another quarter of it they made confession and worshiped the LORD their God. . . . And they cried with a loud voice to the LORD their God. Then the Levites . . . said, "Stand up and bless the LORD your God from everlasting to everlasting. Blessed be Your glorious name, which is exalted above all blessing and praise. You are the LORD, You alone. You have made heaven, the heaven of heavens,

with all their host, the earth and all that is on it,
the seas and all that is in them; and You preserve
all of them; and the host of heaven worships You."
(Nehemiah 9:1–6)

The Israelites assembled in the temple. They humbled themselves before almighty God with a day of general fasting and prayer
and "with earth on their heads," a sign of deep mourning. After
reading the Law for three hours (the Israelites thought in terms
of a twelve-hour day), they confessed their sins and worshiped
for three hours more. I wonder how many minutes out of 180
they gave to confessing their sin as compared to giving praise.
I bet not just five. Worship is not about wallowing in sorrow or
giving a mandatory amount of time to confessing our sins. We
might pray, however, "Dear Lord, it does not feel good to have
You expose my own sin to me. But please do. Teach me to see
and to better understand my sinfulness. Lead me to repentance
and to welcome Your grace *in this fast-fleeting hour!* Fill me with
joy. Capture my heart every day with the heavenly story of Your
Son, the King of all glory, who has come to save me from death
and hell. And let me join with all creation to declare Your great
power and mercy."

Gracious Savior, Grant Your Blessing

1 Gracious Savior, grant Your blessing
To this husband and this wife,
That in peace they live together
In Your love throughout their life.
Christ, defend them from the tempter
And from all that would destroy
Love's foundation You have laid here,
And its threshold paved with joy.

2 Lord, if You are not the builder,
Then the house is built in vain,
For a home without Your presence
Shall without true love remain.
Yet when You within a marriage
Come and dwell with grace divine,
There You fill the empty vessels,
Changing water into wine.

3 Cana's guest, this union hallow;
Tenderly embrace this pair.
Clothe this couple with the garments
They will daily need to wear:
Patience, kindness, and compassion,
Gentleness, humility;
Robe them, Lord, with love to bind them
In a perfect unity.

4 Make their love a living picture
Showing how You loved Your bride:
When You gave Yourself to cleanse her,
When for her You bled and died.
Jesus, You have made her holy,
Pure and fair her radiant train;
To Yourself, Your Church presenting,
Without wrinkle, spot, or stain.

5 Father, You created Adam,
Crafted Eve, and made them one;
Jesus, from their sin You saved us,
As God's true incarnate Son;
Holy Spirit, You forgive us;
From our sins we are released.
Bring us, Lord, at last to heaven,
To the endless wedding feast.

LSB 860
TEXT: STEPHEN P. STARKE, B. 1955;
COPYRIGHT © STEPHEN P. STARKE, ADMIN. CPH

efore us is one of the twenty-first-century hymns included in *LSB*. Matched with a joyful, familiar melody is a beautiful five-stanza wedding prayer asking our gracious Savior to

- grant His blessing to the husband and wife and defend them from the tempter;

- dwell in their house and fill them with grace;

- hallow, embrace, and clothe them with patience (to robe them with love);

- make their love a living picture that shows how He loves His bride; and

- bring us at last to heaven, to the endless wedding feast.

God has never updated His unparalleled design for marriage. These stanzas are new to our hymn corpus, but the meaning stems from unchanging promises God spoke to Adam and Eve in Paradise. The hymn's author succeeds in bringing us face-to-face with a number of marriages spanning thousands of years. The hymn accompanies us at weddings today and also takes us to first-century Cana. It takes us to the marriage of God's Son to His Bride, the Church, and also to Eden. Finally, the hymn takes us to the endless wedding feast in heaven.

In the first stanza, we ask God to grant to the groom and bride a specific blessing. Married couples need Christ's defense *from the tempter*, so part of that defense, part of God's marital blessing, is His holy design for marriage. It is the design He established in the garden before Adam and Eve turned their backs to Him, the holy design Paul describes in Ephesians 5. Because Satan is using culture's ways to terrorize marriages and to undercut our trust in the Lord, we give time in this chapter to defining and defending this blessing from God, His design for marriage.

I wish to recognize Dr. Christopher Mitchell's commentary, *Song of Songs*. It excels at relating the marital love of Solomon and his bride to Christian marriages today, to families, fathers, mothers, and children. The volume also provides biblical commentary on a host of pastoral concerns including infertility, abortion, fornication, and virginity. In addition, Dr. Winger's analysis of Ephesians 5:21b–33 in his commentary may be the most helpful, faithful explanation of God's marital design I have encountered. Much said in these five devotions relating to God's design—wives, submit to your husbands as to the Lord; husbands, love your wives as Christ loved the Church (Ephesians 5:22–25)—stems from the corresponding work of these two servants in their commentaries.

Furthermore, twice in this hymn, the author takes us to Cana (at the end of st. 2 and the beginning of 3). John records the wedding at Cana in 2:1–11. This biblical account is not mostly about the ritual and celebration of the wedding, and it is not mostly about the awe of the water-to-wine miracle, the supernatural work of changing six to nine hundred bottles' worth, dramatic as that is. The first chapter of the Gospel of John introduces John the Baptist, who broadcasts the Lamb of God and His blood for our forgiveness. In chapter 3, the Gospel of John speaks Jesus' saving baptismal language—born of water and the spirit—to Nicodemus. Why does John place a wedding story between John the Baptist's "Lamb of God" proclamation and the baptismal pronouncement to Nicodemus? Dr. Weinrich (*John 1:1–7:1*, 296–325) uncovers the redemptive, cross-centered purpose of the wedding at Cana. Christ does provide our earthly needs, even an abundance of wine for a wedding, but He fills a Christian marriage with much more—His grace.

As couples stand before the Lord's altar, prior to speaking their vows and their being blessed and pronounced married, the pastor reads, "In marriage we see a picture of the communion between Christ and His bride, the Church" (*LSB*, p. 275). Wouldn't you expect to hear it the other way around—"In the communion between Christ and His Bride, we see a picture of marriage, an image of how husbands are to love their wives and how wives are to love and respect their husbands"? However, in Ephesians 5:31–32, Paul teaches that God already had Christ in mind *before* He instituted marriage, and thus instituted marriage in the Garden of Eden to portray what He would do in the future through Christ (Winger, 624–25). In the beginning, God planned for marriage to provide a picture of His self-sacrificing love for us in Christ. This is the mystery the hymn's author places in the fourth stanza, and the devotion dedicated to this stanza approaches it through the story of one husband's loving faithfulness to his wife, who had become *difficult* to love, and through a fourth-century quote regarding our unworthiness to become the Bride of Christ.

Stanza 5 speaks to the Father's creation of Adam and Eve, and that He *made them one*. The devotion addresses marital physical intimacy and comments on the gift of virginity cherished by those whose desire for marriage goes unfulfilled. With thanksgiving to God, the devotion embraces once more God's design for marriage by delineating reasons why we can trust that His design is a blessing. One reason speaks of Christ's subservient role and position before His Father, resulting in our forgiveness and the assurance we have of having our place with God the Father, Son, and Holy Spirit at the endless wedding feast.

> 1   Gracious Savior, grant Your blessing
> To this husband and this wife,
> That in peace they live together
> In Your love throughout their life.
> Christ, defend them from the tempter
> And from all that would destroy
> Love's foundation You have laid here,
> And its threshold paved with joy.

That in Peace They Live Together

God gives a particular blessing that fosters peace in marriage. The blessing is His marital design. To many twenty-first-century Americans, though, this design demeans women. Even some Christian women and men are uncomfortable with the design if they do not understand it. To contemporary ears, it sounds unfair.

> Wives, submit to your own husbands, as to the Lord. For the husband is the head of the wife even as Christ is the head of the church. . . . Husbands, love your wives, as Christ loved the church and gave Himself up for her. (Ephesians 5:22–23, 25)

If I were a wife, I might say, "I'm glad my husband loves me and our children enough to die for us, if such an unimaginable circumstance should ever arise, but how can I 'submit' to him? Am I less important than he is? Does my voice not matter? Am I not an equal partner?"

First, we remember that believing is a gift from God. Because of the gift of faith, we believe many unbelievable things that are said in the Bible. For example, God made water come out of a rock (Exodus 17:6). To think that you would believe this on your own, apart from the Holy Spirit's creating and sustaining faith in your heart through the Means of Grace, is an insult to your natural intelligence. Although one would think that God's design for marriage would sound more natural and believable than the miracles He performed, cultural influences cause many people to struggle with or refuse to believe in the goodness of God's marital design.

The tempter comes with the normal allurements to disturb the peaceful bond between husband and wife and between them and their Lord, and he determines to replace trust in God's design for marriage with doubt. Raising doubt scores a double satanic victory. First, doubting the design works to sabotage marriage. Second, doubting the design works to create doubt in the Designer. If Satan spawns doubt in your heart toward one area of God's good will and work, then his task to lead you to doubt God's Law and love in other areas has become much easier. Ultimately, by blowing around culture's fumes, Satan seeks to destroy our spiritual lungs. He is determined to destroy faith.

God wants love and joy to flourish in marriage; He wants husbands and wives to cherish and delight in each other. But when doubt rises, bad things develop. A wife may be tempted to dominate over her husband or to resent his attempt to lead. A husband may be tempted to carry out his role of headship in a degrading manner, with no humility and love, with no awareness of the tender mercy he receives daily from God. Or he may shy away from his role because of culturally driven misconceptions or because of sheer laziness or selfishness. A sad result is that husbands and wives may express their sinfulness to each other more so than to anyone else.

It may not sound right to our modern ears, but God's marital design is flawless. Difficulty in embracing it comes from misunderstanding the words *submit* or *subordinate*. We can think of it this way—Jesus is subordinate to His Father, but He is not less important. Jesus submitted to God's will by willingly giving up everything for His Bride—for us, His people—in order to save her. God determined that what is good for the Son and the Father, one subordinate to the other though equal in glory and majesty, is also good for husband and wife. The design is not a law given after the fall of man. God gives the marital design His blessing within His creation before sin enters the garden. God's design for marriage is a part of what God saw when He announced, "It is very good." When husbands and wives live in loving service to each other, abiding by God's marital design, they enjoy peace.

Speaking to other husbands, let us love our wives as God's Son loves us. Let us help to make it a joy for them to love us as we model the image of Christ's love.

PRAISE & HONOR — MARRIAGE

> 2 Lord, if You are not the builder,
> Then the house is built in vain,
> For a home without Your presence
> Shall without true love remain.
> Yet when You within a marriage
> Come and dwell with grace divine,
> There You fill the empty vessels,
> Changing water into wine.

Lord, If You Are Not the Builder

I f the Lord is not the marriage builder, why bother with it? God's children cannot imagine making a house into a home without Him. Without Him, marriage is empty. Without Him, *we* are empty. The hymn's author brings us to Cana to see what happens when the Lord dwells within a marriage with divine grace.

> *There You fill the empty vessels,*
> *Changing water into wine.*

John reports that Jesus' mother, His disciples, and Jesus Himself were attending the wedding (John 2:1–11). We read how Mary's mention that they have run out of wine results in Jesus telling the servants to fill to the brim the six stone water jars used for purification And we hear about the amazement of the master who tastes the water now turned to wine. This account is frequently taught as a touching story of Jesus' care for the host family, marking His divine power and His appreciation of celebration. If this is the primary message, wouldn't John have included the people's names? My wife and I attended our niece's wedding, with our four adult children and so many of their cousins together for the first time in years, and with a local brew on

70

tap. It was fun. However, with the wedding at Cana, God points to more than the pleasures He grants on earth.

For every unforgiven man, woman, child, and baby, damnation begins with death and does not end. That is why John does not wait. He brings in Jesus through John the Baptist in chapter 1: "Behold, the Lamb of God who takes away the sin of the world!" (John 1:29). In chapter 3, he unfolds Jesus' promise to Nicodemus and accentuates Holy Baptism: "Truly, truly, I say to you, unless one is born of water and the Spirit, he cannot enter the kingdom of God" (3:5). Why does John place the wedding miracle between John the Baptist pointing to Jesus and Nicodemus pointing to Baptism?

There are clues. First, Jesus gives a strange-sounding, unexpected reply to his mother's notice. She said to Him, "They have no wine." Jesus did not say, "Dear Mother, I will provide." He said, "Woman, . . . My hour has not yet come" (2:4). Jesus was not telling His mother that she cannot tell Him what to do. Jesus' reply may indicate that her statement about wine reminds Him of His Passion. Perhaps He is thinking of Isaiah's heavenly promise of aged wines (Isaiah 25:6–9) and of the marriage feast of the Lamb in His kingdom, which will have no end. In order to welcome the wedding guests at Cana—and all of us—to *that* feast, Jesus knows that the need is much greater than wine. What we need most of all He will secure when He suffers, dies, and rises. The hour for Him to provide it had not yet come.

Second, John tells us that the water jars were there for Jewish rites of purification. Ritual water cannot purify unclean hearts, but the purification water turned to wine points to the greater purification given in the blood of the Lamb, the cleansing, purifying blood of Christ poured over us in the waters of Baptism (John 3). Jesus replaces the ritual water with the cleansing water of His blood (1 John 1:7).

We are empty vessels until Christ purifies us and fills us with His Spirit. Just as He changed the water into wine, He changes our hearts from being self-serving to giving, from obstinate to understanding, from jealous to generous, and from resenting to loving.

PRAISE & HONOR — MARRIAGE

Speaking to other husbands, the Spirit makes our hearts clean and leads us to fulfill our role under God to tenderly care for our wives, that is, to lovingly, sacrificially serve those He has given us to love—just as He has loved us. Headship includes the responsibility to make important decisions for the well-being of our wives and families in those instances when there is not a mutual decision. The foremost responsibility in headship is to bring our wives and families to Jesus and His Word of life to them.

> 3 Cana's guest, this union hallow;
> Tenderly embrace this pair.
> Clothe this couple with the garments
> They will daily need to wear:
> Patience, kindness, and compassion,
> Gentleness, humility;
> Robe them, Lord, with love to bind them
> In a perfect unity.

Robe Them, Lord, with Love to Bind Them

Cana's guest comes to your wedding too. He is attentive, thoughtful, and wise. He is always near, not at shouting distance. He listens well. He follows care and compassion with action. "Fill the jars with water. . . . Now draw some out and take it to the master of the feast" (John 2:7–8). Calling Jesus *Cana's guest* highlights the personal nature of our Lord, who hallowed the couple with His holy presence and, by doing so, honored marriage. Cana's guest was close enough not to allow the day's festive joy to be dimmed for a shortage of wine, and even more, His changing the water to wine emphasizes for every couple the importance of His purifying blood.

Running out of wine is the least of our worries. Standing in judgment with a twenty- or thirty-gallon crock full of sin—now that's a problem. What Cana's guest would do for us at the cross is the ultimate solution. Yet it is wonderfully comforting to know that He is present at the wedding of every Christian couple and is with them each day thereafter in the living power of His Word. Cana's guest came down from above, incarnate by the Holy Spirit, to bless the womb of His mother and their home, to touch lepers, to command demons, to refute Satan, to shun temptation, to heal, raise, and forgive. He took action for others while on the way to His own death, the act that, above all others, makes Cana's guest the one we most need.

Mary was not shy in approaching Cana's guest. He invites us to do likewise. He answered the request of His mother on behalf of the wedding family at Cana. It is important to ask Him to make holy and loving each married couple, and to tenderly provide them with all they will need to live together in holy love.

Having Cana's guest dwell in our homes sounds wonderful! But what happens after a few years, after the blush wears off? Is the national divorce rate lower for Christians? It's interesting how cohabitating couples answer this question during premarital counseling: Why did you decide to live together before marrying? "It's a matter of finances" is a common answer, as if to justify sin for the love of money. Some answer that they fear divorce. They've been through it already, or a brother was, or their best friend is going through it, or their parents were. The goal of securing a solid marriage is commendable, of course. How unfortunate, unwise, and unfaithful, however, to attempt to do so by discarding God's Word and marital design. Most couples genuinely desire God's blessing. They know they need Christ. They want their children to grow up with a strong faith. They desire the Lord's Supper. They fear divorce.

It is a good fear to have. But protection against divorce, unhappiness, and bitterness does not come from cohabitating ahead of time. Fulfillment and joy in marriage come from trusting God and His design, from consciously living it out every day, and by putting on the proper clothing received from Cana's guest—patience, kindness, compassion, gentleness, and humility.

No one leaves home without dressing for the occasion. Likewise, a husband and wife approaching the day without putting on *patience, kindness, and compassion, Gentleness, humility,* as the hymn says, leave ugliness fully exposed. The hymn's author is the shepherd of a parish full of God's people. He knows and prays: *Clothe this couple with the garments they will daily need to wear.* Daily, in any kind of marital weather, gentleness and humility and the entire outfit look good and wear well. When we do act out selfishly, we say, "I am sorry," and gladly remind each other that Cana's guest not only blessed marriage with His presence and wine making but also pointed us to Himself. He forgives us and keeps us. He dresses us to love and serve each day with gladness and wraps us with an invaluable piece of cloth to hold us in unity: His love.

> 4 Make their love a living picture
> Showing how You loved Your bride:
> When You gave Yourself to cleanse her,
> When for her You bled and died.
> Jesus, You have made her holy,
> Pure and fair her radiant train;
> To Yourself, Your Church presenting,
> Without wrinkle, spot, or stain.

Make Their Love
a Living Picture

His wife was depressed. His love for her was genuine and humbling to see. It was not that she was no longer beautiful in his eyes; it was that she was no longer kind. Her mind restricted her ability to love and engage. They seldom left home. When they did, he would always include his wife when interacting with friends, but he made no apologies for her and showed no uneasiness, even though her replies were often despondent or terse. It was as if he was the only one who did not see how difficult she could be.

The life he had and the wife he married had both changed drastically three decades earlier. A tragedy caused the depression that led to the guilt and the shame she felt for being unable to get past it. "The door to her heart is jammed shut," he said. "She does not really come out and will not let me in." He wondered if she refused to acknowledge his love because she thought she was unable to give it in return and would feel even more guilt.

I did not know what to say. He smiled and said, "Pastor, I know she would treat me even better were the roles reversed, 'for better, for worse, in sickness and in health.' We took our vows to heart."

I did not respond. He asked, "What are you thinking?" I replied, "Well, seeing your love for your wife teaches me something about what Paul meant. 'Husbands, love your wives, as Christ loved the church and gave Himself up for her'" (Ephesians 5:25).

Make their love a living picture Showing how You loved Your bride, we sing earnestly in stanza 4. In the Bible, God uses marriage as the image for His loving relationship to us. Attraction is the opening component of our marriages. There are a host of words, including *genuine, content, pretty,* and *practical,* to describe why I was thankful to God for my bride. You can generate your word list too.

That it is not how it was for Jesus, the Bridegroom, in choosing us to be His Bride. By conception, all people inherit Adam and Eve's sinfulness. All are born separated from God, without the desire, without the ability to love and be faithful to Him (Romans 5:12; 7:18). People think that they are lovable. They are blind to their faults and unaware of the depth of sin in their hearts (Matthew 15:19). Even so, God speaks to us words such as "I will betroth you to Me forever. I will betroth you to Me . . . in steadfast love and in mercy" (Hosea 2:19). God created an image of His love for us, His Bride, when He instructed His prophet Hosea to "Go, take to yourself a wife of whoredom" (1:2). Hosea did, and she repeated her offenses. He continued to love her. Our natures are warped so badly that we may not see our shortcomings easily identified by everyone else. Regarding our unworthiness to become the Bride of Christ, a fourth-century Christian teacher expresses it this way:

> Come, then, let me talk to you as I would speak to a bride about to be led into the holy nuptial chamber. Let me give you, too, a glimpse of the Bridegroom's exceeding wealth and of the ineffable kindness which He shows to His bride. Let me point out to her the sordid past from which she is escaping and the glorious future she is about to enjoy. . . . He does not have her come to Him as His bride because He has longed for her

comeliness, or her beauty, or the bloom of her body. On the contrary, the bride He has brought into the nuptial chamber is deformed and ugly, thoroughly and shamefully sordid, and, practically, wallowing in the very mire of her sins. (Chrysostom, quoted in Weinrich, 313)

At the opening of this devotion, I shared the story of the man whose love grew for his wife, who suffered from debilitating depression; we heard from Chrysostom from the Early Church; and we read about Hosea's unconditional love recorded in Scripture. All of these examples depict God's love for us. Our love for our spouse is an image to others of God's love for us. Marital love is part of God's evangelism plan to communicate with those who do not know Christ's love. True, others may not know that Jesus is the source and model of love in Christian marriage, but maybe a couple's strong marital bond will attract enough attention to cause someone to ask, "Why is there so much love in your marriage?" Then one can answer, "Well, because Christ has forgiven us so much and given us so much love." To love your spouse for better, for worse, in sickness, and in health establishes a living picture that reflects how the Lord loves His Bride, you.

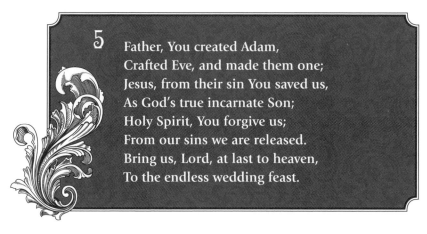

5
Father, You created Adam,
Crafted Eve, and made them one;
Jesus, from their sin You saved us,
As God's true incarnate Son;
Holy Spirit, You forgive us;
From our sins we are released.
Bring us, Lord, at last to heaven,
To the endless wedding feast.

And Made Them One

In a most intimate expression of the union God made, two do become one. God's perfect design for marriage includes purity and monogamy. It is heartbreaking that society has stolen innocence from children, expressing and demanding complete disregard for the beautiful gift of virginity that God bestows, the gift which in turn is given only once, to only one. Those children of God called to keep their virginity throughout their lives do not squander it but look forward to returning it honorably to their Creator and Bridegroom. (See Mitchell, *Song of Songs*, 203.)

When we succumb to self-serving temptation, there is forgiveness. There is also opportunity for us to impress deeply upon the hearts of younger people what is good, clean, beautiful, helpful, and honorable, and to sharply contrast it with what is sinful, filthy, selfish, harmful, and regrettable. The joy and goodness of passionate, marital intimacy is something about which God is not ashamed and you need not be.

And made them one in the hymn refers to more than the physical union of husband and wife. This phrase encompasses the God-designed substance of marriage, without which the one-flesh union means nothing. The foundation of marriage is God's love for them in Christ, and it includes their fear of, love for, and trust in Him. This marital design is identified by the headship afforded to the husband and by the subordination entrusted to the wife. Here are reasons why you can trust God and His design, regardless of what today's culture insists:

- God crafted Eve from Adam's rib, not apart from him, not from dirt as He did Adam. God designed her to be a helper fit for him and brought her to him. Being a helper does not mean being beneath or unequal any more than the psalmist believed he was above the Creator when he prayed, "I lift up my eyes to the hills. From where does my help come? My help comes from the LORD, who made heaven and earth" (Psalm 121:1–2).

- The role of wifely subordination parallels the Lord's subservient role to His Father. The Father and the Son together with the Spirit share equal glory and eternal majesty. That is not trivial. Jesus is equal to the Father with respect to His divinity but less than the Father with respect to His humanity. Take a moment to review the Athanasian Creed on pages 319–20 of *Lutheran Service Book*.

- Women are not called or created to be subordinate to all men. "Wives, submit to *your own* husbands, as to the Lord" (Ephesians 5:22, emphasis added). The God-blessed roles of subordination and headship, carefully defined, are for a wife and husband in marriage.

- God does not say or even suggest that wives are inferior to husbands, that they are less capable, unwise, or worth less to Him than husbands. It could be argued that they are worth more, based on the role assigned to husbands, who are to give up their lives for their wives and children if called to do so.

Many people refuse to accept that God can position the husband with headship and the wife as subordinate, and still sustain equal worth and value between them. When Christians speak in support of marriage as God lovingly defined it, men may be accused of misogyny—of hating women—and women may be accused of not being able to think for themselves. If Jesus had gone with the current of our times instead of trusting His Father's will, He would never have come down, would have refused the role of sacrificial Savior, and Paul would not have been able to write of our Lord, "who, though He was in the form of God, did not count equality with God a thing to be grasped, but emptied Himself, by taking the form of a servant, being born in the likeness of men" (Philippians 2:6–7). The point here is not what Jesus *did* as a servant up to and including His crucifixion. *That* point actually speaks to the role of husband to live with sacrificial love. Rather, the point is Jesus' willingness *to be* subservient to the Father. Here Jesus provides a pattern for both wives and husbands. Wives model Christ's willing submission to His Father. Husbands model Christ's sacrificial love for His Bride.

Husbands and wives love and serve each other, according to God's design and in keeping with their abilities, cherishing each other without the need for personal gain or reward. This is because Christ the Bridegroom has given to us, His Bride, all things unto everlasting life.

Rock of Ages, Cleft for Me

1 Rock of Ages, cleft for me,
Let me hide myself in Thee;
Let the water and the blood,
From Thy riven side which flowed,
Be of sin the double cure:
Cleanse me from its guilt and pow'r.

2 Not the labors of my hands
Can fulfill Thy Law's demands;
Could my zeal no respite know,
Could my tears forever flow,
All for sin could not atone;
Thou must save, and Thou alone.

3 Nothing in my hand I bring;
Simply to Thy cross I cling.
Naked, come to Thee for dress;
Helpless, look to Thee for grace;
Foul, I to the fountain fly;
Wash me, Savior, or I die.

4 While I draw this fleeting breath,
When mine eyelids close in death,
When I soar to worlds unknown,
See Thee on Thy judgment throne,
Rock of Ages, cleft for me,
Let me hide myself in Thee.

LSB 761
TEXT: AUGUSTUS M. TOPLADY (1740–78)

ach stanza in this much-loved hymn announces a theme. Jesus' blood cures me from sin (st. 1). My efforts and emotions get me nowhere against God's Law (st. 2). I cannot assist in the saving. I have nothing. I am less than nothing (st. 3). And when my eyes close at last, there will be a horrific awakening, unless He intervenes (st. 4).

The hymn uses easily understood images and Bible references to reflect the worshiper's desperation and to bring relief in Christ. Strong words such as *cleft, hide, zeal, tears, naked, helpless, foul* impact us. The use of simple rhyme at the end of every couplet is effective. And most certainly, another strong feature is the sturdy, endearing metaphor for God—*Rock of Ages*. It permeates the entire four-stanza prayer, although we sing the title only twice. *Rock of Ages* is a strong image that contrasts with a sinner's helplessness. Let's look at the biblical image.

Rock of Ages

- The psalmist urges us to "make a joyful noise to the rock of our salvation!" (Psalm 95:1)

- David knows the source of his rescue from death and his enemies, calling the Lord his rock. (2 Samuel 22:47)

- A fitting verse to mark confirmation vows is Psalm 18:2. It expresses the security granted to those who know the Lord is their rock.

Crevices, cliffs, rocky crags, which may be foreign images to a Midwestern pastor, were not foreign for God's children of ancient times. They served as vantage points in battle, as hideaways when attacked. Nonetheless, it is not the physical rock or high mountain that saves. David knows this. The psalmists know. "I lift up my eyes to the hills. From where does my help come?" (121:1). Not from the mountain, but from the Maker (Psalm 121:2), for "He alone is my rock and my salvation, my fortress; I shall not be greatly shaken" (62:2).

The Old Testament frequently demonstrates God's saving action through real rock formations, but Paul ties it to the spiritual rock of Christ, from whom all believers from all times receive spiritual food and drink (1 Corinthians 10:1–4). *Rock of Ages* is a reassuring image. But of course our Savior is not granite. He has flesh and blood. Ultimately, the rock that saves is the rock that bleeds (John 19:34).

Phrases such as *Let me hide myself in Thee* and *Simply to Thy cross I cling* are comforting when we are weighed down with dejection, stress, loneliness, and grief at the death of a loved one or at the thought of our own. The story has been told of the hymnwriter's dire circumstance—his confrontation with death by storm—serving as his prayer's inspiration. In the hymn, the author, however, does not pray about comfort regarding life's problems or about death in relation to fear or grief. He prays about one thing—sin. In the first three stanzas, he pleads for rescue from sin's threat against him. When he mentions death in stanza 4, it is the precursor to divine judgment. Facing death brings into focus the greatest crisis: *See Thee on Thy judgment throne.* As the author prays, he is not so concerned with dejection, stress, and death. He is concerned about hell. The following phrases say so:

Let me hide myself in Thee.

Be of sin the double cure.

Not the labors of my hands.

All for sin could not atone.

Thou must save, and Thou alone.

Helpless, look to Thee for grace.

Foul, I to the fountain fly.

Wash me, Savior, or I die.

See Thee on Thy judgment throne.

Rock of Ages, cleft for me,

Let me hide myself in Thee.

"Rock of Ages" is a hymn of hope and comfort for every guilty sinner who sees judgment at death's door because it carries us to the Rock of salvation.

Speaking of judgment, although hymns with a sure message of mercy, such as "Rock of Ages," invite confession of sin, why is our approach to repentance and confession in worship sometimes halfhearted? Is it because reading or reciting a general confession of sins fails to ignite feelings? We are tempted to equate feelings in worship with blessings from God. Good feelings, we think, mean that God is blessing us, and we may leave church thankful for such an uplifting worship experience. Conversely, no feelings mean God is not blessing us, and we may leave church feeling empty, thinking we did not get anything out of it. Such thinking discounts the power of the Gospel, spoken and administered when we are gathered in the Lord's house. I may not feel anything or differently after hearing the words of absolution. My emotions may or may not be stirred at the receiving of Christ's body and blood, but we can thank God that the reality of Christ's gifts to us in Word and Sacrament is not dependent upon how we feel. We help ourselves by focusing less on emotion and more on confession—confession of all that Scripture says Jesus is, did, and does, and confession of our sin. When we sing "Rock of Ages," we do both; we confess our desperate need *and* His steadfast, solid-as-a-rock mercy and love. Whether or not good feelings come, the blessings we receive from the Rock of Ages never end.

Music and Meter Help the Message

Speak the following stanza aloud, accenting the syllables in all caps.

> ROCK of A-ges, CLEFT for ME,
> LET me HIDE mySELF in THEE
> LET the WAter AND the BLOOD,
> FROM Thy RIVen SIDE which FLOWED
> BE of SIN the DOUble CURE:
> CLEANSE me FROM its GUILT and POW'r.

In trochaic lines, every other syllable is accented, beginning with the first. Accents often land on important words. The repeating and falling rhythm creates a pulsating sound that can be dramatic, but if it goes on too long, it becomes tiresome. The melody enhances the mood established by the trochaic rhythm. It helps carry the message to our hearts. Initially, I was drawn to the steep interval between the fourth and fifth notes, the first note corresponding to the second syllable of *Ages,* and the second to *cleft,* and associated with it a sense of crying out to the Lord for mercy. A former music professor commented to me via email: "The tune has a lot of upward gestures, one in every phrase, and they all suggest to me a sense of anguish. It is a very emotional hymn" (email from Dr. John Eggert, July 8, 2018). The hymn presents another opportunity to thank the Lord for the gift of music.

> **1** Rock of Ages, cleft for me,
> Let me hide myself in Thee;
> Let the water and the blood,
> From Thy riven side which flowed,
> Be of sin the double cure:
> Cleanse me from its guilt and pow'r.

Let Me Hide Myself in Thee

The author makes no mention of finding rescue from death in the cleft of the Rock. He wants to hide from the guilt and power of sin, not simply from life's end. He calls God the *Rock of Ages*, and he knows the safest place to be: with the *Rock*, the God-man from whom water and blood flowed as the guards who pierced Him looked on (John 19:34, 36–37). Then the plea: *Be of sin the double cure.* What does this mean?

We need a cure from sin's guilt and power, as the author attests in this stanza's final line. The cure comes from the One who was pierced. The cure comes by way of substitution. John saw guards break the legs of the other two crucified criminals to ensure their death. He saw them come to Jesus, recognize His death, and realize that no bone-breaking was needed, though a soldier speared His side to make certain. What happened next? John saw the water and blood (John 19:32–34). "He who saw it has borne witness—his testimony is true, and he knows that he is telling the truth—that you also may believe" (v. 35). John knows. He wants us to believe. Jesus' sinless life and death, His water and blood, cleanse us from sin's guilt and power. He took our guilt into Himself—cure number 1. He released us from sin's power to accuse us according to the Law—cure number 2. If Jesus took our guilt, the Law cannot say to the Judge, "He's guilty!

Give him what he deserves!" *Be of sin the double cure: Cleanse me from its guilt and power.*

The problem is I keep sinning; I can't stop. And guilt hovers around me. How does it go for you? *Double cure* reminds me of Isaiah's shocking words of God's determination to deliver double comfort to His people and double pardon for their sin. The Lord is emphatic:

> Comfort, comfort My people, says your God.
> Speak tenderly to Jerusalem, and cry to her that
> her warfare is ended, that her iniquity is pardoned,
> that she has received from the LORD's hand double
> for all her sins. (Isaiah 40:1–2)

The author of our hymn faced death. He was moved to cry for mercy and knew it rested with the Rock of Ages. Isaiah pronounced God's double comfort to His people after first humbling them with a history-changing, stinging blast of Law. Babylon obliterated the holy city, Jerusalem, in 587 BC. Israel faced annihilation. The Israelites must have wondered if the Lord had determined not to rescue them because they had rejected Him. They knew they were at fault.

But in Isaiah's day and still today, God cannot bear the thought of losing His children, who turn to other gods that cannot cleanse us, cannot save us. Our Lord corrects us and even punishes us to humble us, to turn us, and to restore to us the joy of salvation that only He can provide. The Lord commands His heavenly council to "comfort, comfort My people," and with a double portion of mercy, with unexpected, undeserved, and unmatched faithfulness, God heals and restores. He does not wait for us to straighten out or pay up. No, while we were still sinning, Christ died for us (Romans 5:8). We cannot stop our flow of sin. And He would not keep from us His double cure.

2 Not the labors of my hands
Can fulfill Thy Law's demands;
Could my zeal no respite know,
Could my tears forever flow,
All for sin could not atone;
Thou must save, and Thou alone.

Thou Must Save,
and Thou Alone

We can never give what the Law demands of us. There are no mulligans in the game of life. Do-overs are not allowed. Every shot, every play, every move counts. We must keep the Law. When pressed for an example of the Law, Jesus said, "You shall love the Lord your God with all your heart and with all your soul and with all your mind" (Matthew 22:37). *All* is a big word. How much of your heart, soul, and mind, how much of your energy and strength, is the Lord receiving from you at home, at work, uptown, or at church? Paul knew that afflictions and imprisonment awaited him in every city. He told the Ephesians, "I do not account my life of any value nor as precious to myself" (Acts 20:24).

What would our lives look like if we joined Paul in saying that? He completed his thought, "If only I may finish my course and the ministry that I received from the Lord Jesus, to testify to the gospel of the grace of God" (20:24). Enjoying life is not against God's will. Living selfishly is. Paul was most interested in loving God and his neighbor. He was not shy about teaching others everything God says, to warn and to comfort, to convict and to forgive, and he was eager to help them with earthly needs too. Paul tells us to imitate him. And he quoted Jesus, "It is more blessed to give than to receive" (20:35). Read the moving account in Acts 20:17–38. It encourages me to want to do more and helps me see how much of my *all* I'm holding back. And that brings us back to the hymn, to the Law's demands. Failure to meet them doesn't mean we shouldn't try or that in Christ we do not have ample motivation to do so. It means we have a big problem. This stanza cites three weak alternatives to fix it.

First is *labor,* or good works. Are you the kind of person who, although you know you are sinful and fully forgiven in Christ, think you are a little better than others because of all the good you do? that somehow this makes a difference? That's like saying you are closer to Mars just because you are standing a stairstep ahead of the guy behind you.

Zeal is number 2 on the list. With that word, the author was likely combating some bad theology, bad biblical teaching of his day. We might hear *zeal* to mean "passion," as in being passionate about the Lord and faith and living it. Nothing wrong with that! However, when my zeal for Christ, for learning, for sharing my faith, for giving, helping, and sacrificing, for trying to make a difference in people's lives like Paul did causes me to think I don't need Christ as much as I used to or as much as others who are not so zealous, then I've succeeded only in placing myself on a step next to the guy in the paragraph above. Mars is a long way away. Frankly, the Lord is much more passionate about His Law than you are about keeping it. Your zeal is no answer for His demands.

Is anyone you know tempted to cry their way to heaven? Tears, the third alternative, do not help. When we are brought to tears by guilt, it's a good indication that our guilt has moved us closer to Christ and His blood and that our faith has been rekindled a bit. But tears do not make up for anything. Tears do not soak up sin, do not atone. We know this. We know we need something else. The hymn assures us *Thou must save, and Thou alone.* It is so true: "You, O Lord, must save, and You alone. Dear Lord Jesus, thank You for saving me."

> 3   Nothing in my hand I bring;
> Simply to Thy cross I cling.
> Naked, come to Thee for dress;
> Helpless, look to Thee for grace;
> Foul, I to the fountain fly;
> Wash me, Savior, or I die.

Nothing in My Hand I Bring

*G*od hears you sing. How might His conversation with you go after singing this stanza? God doesn't talk to us directly, of course. We do have His Word in Holy Scripture. But as a way to help consider the message of this stanza, without wanting to be silly, imagine Him speaking to you. If you happen to be a person who struggles to keep from loving things, maybe He would say:

> You are holding your hand tightly behind your back. Yes, I know what it is without asking because I am all-knowing. Remember Psalm 139:7–16. Show Me what you are hiding. The hymn's author is not talking about worldly things when he says *Nothing in my hand I bring.* This stanza is not about the things My children are tempted to love and trust more than Me. The author means that your efforts and offerings will not help you when I come to judge you. However, many people are not concerned about My grace to cover their sin. Many are searching for a good feeling. If he wrote today, the author would not begin the stanza as he did. He would write *My own hands now full of things, To Thy cross I do not cling.* Back to My question: What is in your hand?

We can't know what the author would write today. Some of us sing his hymn sincerely because of its message. We may have recited hundreds of times "By grace you have been saved through faith" (Ephesians 2:8) and heard dozens of sermons proclaiming forgiveness, but still doubt whether we are forgiven. For us, no substitute wording is needed! We know we have nothing to offer God to make up for our sins! *Simply to Thy cross I cling!* However, I took liberty to adjust the stanza's meaning because others of us may take God's grace for granted, much the same as we do sunshine and clean water. The rewrite of the stanza's opening gives us something to consider. What do you crave too much? God does not want you to let go of the cross, which is to say, He does not want you to let go of Christ. When you cling tightly to something in this world, without admitting it to God—with no intention of loosening your grip—it may be time to sing "To Thy cross I do not cling." To use a different analogy, it is like a man pretending that his misplaced love and emotion for a woman at work is not stealing his love for his wife and weakening their marriage. Let's redirect to the cross. "Those who cling to worthless idols turn away from God's love for them" (Jonah 2:8 NIV).

This is also true: you do not need to fear confessing your sin to God or to your pastor. Pastors are ordained servants of God. They speak His words, "I forgive you all your sins, in the name of the Father and of the Son and of the Holy Spirit."

This is also true: clinging to the cross is good. If, however, the words in this stanza—*cling, come, look, fly*—seem to put too much emphasis on your action, if you fear you cannot hold on to Christ's cross tightly enough, there is another way to think about these phrases:

> *Naked, come to Thee for dress;*
> *Helpless, look to Thee for grace;*
> *Foul, I to the fountain fly;*
> *Wash me, Savior, or I die!*

All the imagery is baptismal. In Baptism, the Lord is working, not the one being baptized. In Baptism, the Lord clothes you with Christ, pours grace over you, and washes you. You will not die eternally!

4 While I draw this fleeting breath,
When mine eyelids close in death,
When I soar to worlds unknown,
See Thee on Thy judgment throne,
Rock of Ages, cleft for me,
Let me hide myself in Thee.

See Thee on Thy
Judgment Throne

To help capture the intensity of seeing God *on Thy judgment throne*, of what awaits this world when His fearful, earthshaking presence as Judge is revealed, read the following short passages:

- Revelation 6:12–17

- Revelation 16:17–21

- Revelation 20:11–15

- Ezekiel 28:17–23

The end of this world is so terrifying, even the "earth and sky" flee (Revelation 20:11). When John sees stars falling from heaven like figs shaken off a tree and a shaking of the earth so violent that the islands and mountains move or vanish (6:13–14), it is time for people of every rank and trade, the wealthy and wanting, naysayers, doubters, and those fallen away, to hide. They cry out, pleading with the mountains and rocks to cover them, to hide them from the face of the One sitting on the throne (6:15–17). John sees fear and panic everywhere, a terror more unyielding and intense than has ever come upon man. Lightning flashes, deafening thunder, tremors, and then the undreamed-of, enormous hailstones, one hundred pounds each, slam into the earth and crush people; *See Thee on Thy judgment throne.*

Cities are demolished; the earth's surface is obliterated. And let's not get stuck on the question of whether some or all of the catastrophic action literally or figuratively depicts the wrath of God. When we *See Thee on Thy judgment throne,* humanity's sin meets God's wrath. The time of sorrow and repentance has passed. It will be too late. All who rejected the Lamb may attempt escape but have nowhere to go. Justice comes. Every person, the entire human race, stands before the large throne. Even the sea gives up the dead (20:13). No one misses a turn. John forewarned, "An hour is coming when all who are in the tombs will hear His voice and come out" (John 5:28–29). Two things fill the scene: the Judge seated on the large throne and all people—every one ever born—standing before Him (Brighton, 172–73).

Are we really that bad? So many Christians strive to live for Him and for others. Three decades of pastoral ministry have humbled and uplifted me as I have observed God's children sacrifice, serve, give, encourage, and more. Even so, throughout our lifetimes, we did not recognize many of our sins, or they were discounted, denied, or forgotten. God recognizes, counts, and remembers. Books are for keeping record (Jeremiah 32:8–14; Daniel 7:10), and God has record books of the whole lives of all who faced the light of day, including you. "The '*books*' are a visual representation of God's indelible and unerring mind and remembrance" (Brighton, 583).

> And I saw the dead, great and small, standing before the throne, and books were opened. . . . And the dead were judged by what was written in the books, according to what they had done. (Revelation 20:12)

This past week, talking to a church member about "Rock of Ages" and Revelation 20, he said, "Pastor, I know some things I've done. How is this really going to go?"

"You and me both," I confessed. "How this is going to go, praise God, is we are going to thank Him for having written our names in that other book."

> Then another book was opened, which is the book
> of life. (Revelation 20:12)

Your name written in that book means everything. God has written your name in His heart. He chose you in Him before He formed the world (Ephesians 1:4). He washed you in Jesus' blood through Baptism. True, all are judged on the basis of what is in the *books*, but while unbelievers are judged as guilty and punished accordingly, God's Word promises repeatedly that Christians are declared innocent, are forgiven. In fact, amazingly, wonderfully, our sinful deeds are not recorded in the *books*, for only our good deeds are written there (Matthew 25:31–46). Our sins will never be uncovered. God promises, "I will remember [your] sins no more" (Hebrews 8:12). And "though your sins are like scarlet, they shall be white as snow" (Isaiah 1:18), and He has removed our sins from us "as far as the east is from the west" (Psalm 103:12). They are buried with Christ, because through Baptism God buried you with Him (Colossians 2:12).

Let All Mortal Flesh Keep Silence

1 Let all mortal flesh keep silence
And with fear and trembling stand;
Ponder nothing earthly-minded,
For with blessing in His hand
Christ our God to earth descending
Comes our homage to demand.

2 King of kings yet born of Mary,
As of old on earth He stood,
Lord of lords in human vesture,
In the body and the blood,
He will give to all the faithful
His own self for heav'nly food.

3 Rank on rank the host of heaven
Spreads its vanguard on the way
As the Light of Light, descending
From the realms of endless day,
Comes the pow'rs of hell to vanquish
As the darkness clears away.

4 At His feet the six-winged seraph,
Cherubim with sleepless eye,
Veil their faces to the presence
As with ceaseless voice they cry:
"Alleluia, alleluia!
Alleluia, Lord Most High!"

LSB 621
TEXT: LITURGY OF ST. JAMES, FIFTH CENTURY
TRANSLATION: GERARD MOULTRIE (1829–85), ALT.

et All Mortal Flesh Keep Silence" pulls together Christians spanning a host of centuries. The original words, a component of what is known as the Liturgy of St. James, were written in Greek and used in Jerusalem in the beginning of the fifth century. They were chanted in preparation for the Lord's Supper. Hundreds of years later, in the mid-nineteenth century, a chaplain from Bristol translated and paraphrased the Greek liturgical text into English. Then, in the early twentieth century, the hymn was paired with a seventeenth-century French melody, making the rich and beautiful musical offering found in hymnals across denominations today.

For me, singing a paraphrase of the words heard by God's people in Jerusalem nearly 1,600 years ago elicits a strong sense of reverence. Realizing that the hymn has given testament to the power and grace of Christ across continents for 1.5 millennia causes me to question whether a devotion is needed to further enhance it. Yet with key words and phrases, the hymn invites reverence and thanksgiving before the Lord and also meditation. The first two lines are a perfect example. *Let all mortal flesh keep silence And with fear and trembling stand.* Are we not in church? What about joy and gladness? Is not God on our side, full of grace and abounding in love? In the opening devotion, we will explore the first stanza's concepts: *mortal flesh, fear and trembling, ponder nothing earthly, blessing in His hand, Christ our God.* They speak to the essence of worship.

Before then, though, we take a moment to reflect on *silence.* This hymn associates it with weekly worship, with our scheduled time to be still before the Lord with fear, love, and trust in Him, when we revere and praise Him, hear Him in His Word, and receive His gifts of salvation. There are also unscheduled times when God brings us into silence, causing us to long for His Word to break through.

In the corridor of a hospital emergency room, more than twenty high school students stared numbly or broke down with intense emotion because another student, a few feet away, lay comatose with tubes and machines helping to sustain her life. The pastor who sat with them shifted focus to *nothing earthly-*

minded and after talking about their friend, her family, and what she meant to them, said, "Yes, the Lord could have prevented this accident, and He can bring healing or a miracle. The Creator can do that, and we are going to ask Him to. We also see how serious her condition is, so we are going to remember that Jesus came into His world, into our lives all fouled up by sin and death, not to guarantee that we all live a long life. We are all in shock because this is not a good situation. So remember why Jesus came. He came to grab the cross for two reasons. He took the cross to pay the penalty for our sins, and He took the cross to triumph over death. To defeat death is not to avoid it. Jesus could have avoided it. To defeat death is to die and then rise to life. That is what He did. That is Easter. He took the judgment and penalty for our sins, and then for you and your friend and for me He totally overpowered death." When the Lord uses life's sharp turns to silence us, to turn us to Him, we are most ready to receive *the blessing in His hand* and to recognize the purpose of His descent from heaven to earth.

Stanza 2 beautifully weaves the presence of God in Mary's Son with the sacramental presence of Christ's body and blood in the Holy Supper. Stanza 3 assures us that the mighty army of angels and the power of God conquer the powers of hell. And in stanza 4, we join with angels, seraphim and cherubim, into the visions of heaven, to where Christ is ascended, visible now only through faith's eye, singing the alleluias without end.

In the devotions, we will highlight original Greek words and phrases from this ancient preparatory hymn for the Lord's Supper that correspond to the same Greek words and phrases used in the New Testament writings. The Church has always set Scripture texts to music in the liturgy or based components of the Divine Service and of other orders of worship squarely on the Word of God.

> 1 Let all mortal flesh keep silence
> And with fear and trembling stand;
> Ponder nothing earthly-minded,
> For with blessing in His hand
> Christ our God to earth descending
> Comes our homage to demand.

Let All Mortal Flesh Keep Silence

hy did the fifth-century Greek liturgy upon which the hymn is based use the words *Let all mortal flesh* instead of saying simply "Let everybody"? The word choice is a matter of theological truth, not literary style. There is one type of human flesh. The adjective in the Greek liturgy captures it. *Mortal* means "certain to die." *Mortal* means "fatal." We hear about mortality rates—infant mortality rates, neonatal mortality rates—and aren't they all a little misleading, as if those who live a long life have defied mortality? No one defies mortality. I am reminded each time I turn in or out of our driveway. My wife and I live in the country, directly across from a cemetery. *Let all mortal flesh keep silence*—let us hear the saving Word from the God of life.

And with fear and trembling stand.

When God roared, His children would come trembling from the west (Hosea 11:10). The Lord will look upon the one who is contrite in spirit and who trembles at His Word (Isaiah 66:2), the psalmist's flesh trembles for fear of the Lord (Psalm 119:120), and a woman with great faith came trembling and fell down before Him (Luke 8:47). Even the mountains, recognizing God's rebuke, tremble (Job 26:11). Solomon stresses this theme in at least ten different chapters in Proverbs—the fear of the Lord is the beginning of wisdom (1; 2; 8; 9; 10; 14; 15; 19; 22; 31).

One more—the Corinthians received Titus with *fear and trembling*. Titus was a pastor. Titus was not Jesus. He was a Greek, but he was not a Greek god. So why receive him with *fear and trembling*? Titus was delivering the Word of God from the apostle Paul to the Corinthians (2 Corinthians 7:13–15). Their *fear and trembling* marked their fear of, love for, and trust in God and His Word proclaimed to them by His servant.

In the Old Testament, sometimes *fear* means "fear." Frankly, when our sinful nature is trying to make decisions, we need to fear God's wrath. Often, *fear* means "trust," as in Psalm 130:3–4: "If You, O LORD, should mark iniquities, O Lord, who could stand? But with You there is forgiveness, that You may be feared." *Fear* can mean "clinging to the Lord," and if we could fear the Lord perfectly, we would have no other fears (Psalm 34:4). Those who step before Him with indifference or who dare step past Him with no *fear and trembling* live dangerously.

The opening lines of this stanza sound like a warning for what must be coming. They are not, for *Christ our God* has descended *with blessing in His hand*. We may come in silence and with deep trust because of the gifts He brings. One of my seminary professors loved to teach, to exalt Christ's work among us, with simple sentences that thicken and mature with time and meditation:

- Salvation achieved by Christ alone is ours by His gift alone.

- His ways of giving are His to determine as He pleases. Only thus are they sure and liberating in their bestowal of what He says He is giving.

- We may in no way make His means of grace subject to our determinations.

- His are the words we are given to proclaim.

- His is the name put on us with the water of Baptism.

- His is the body and blood, which He gives into our mouths to eat and to drink.

- His is the forgiveness bestowed with the words of absolution.

- His are the keys entrusted to His ministry. (Sasse, 9)

[He] comes our homage to demand.

God did not come to earth to demand honor. The hymn does not mean that. He could have demanded our praise without coming down, without stiff-arming His way past temptation to earn the right to carry the cross of judgment for us. He could have demanded our praise without conquering death and hell. The homage that brings Him the greatest honor is our receiving the gifts of salvation He desires to give. He comes *with blessing in His hand.*

> Take, eat; this is the true body of our Lord and
> Savior Jesus Christ, given into death for your sins.
> Take, drink; this is the true blood of our Lord and
> Savior Jesus Christ, shed for the forgiveness of your
> sins. (*LSB*, p. 164)

The everlasting blessing He brings elicits the homage we give.

2

King of kings yet born of Mary,
As of old on earth He stood,
Lord of lords in human vesture,
In the body and the blood,
He will give to all the faithful
His own self for heav'nly food.

In the Body and the Blood: Slaughtered

ere it not for this phrase—*in the body and the blood*—we'd wonder why the translator would omit a key word from the Greek hymn. The word is *slaughtered* or *slain*. In the liturgy, they sang: *The King of kings and Lord of lords, Christ our God, is coming to be slaughtered.* That phrase was chanted as the elements for the Lord's Supper were brought forward to the altar. The essence of *slaughtered* is captured by *in the body and the blood.* For you and for me there is no body and blood given as sacrifice, *His own self for heav'nly food,* if He were not slaughtered like a lamb.

Recall the essence of Old Testament animal sacrifices. Lambs were slaughtered by the thousands each year on the observation of the Passover, the holy day of deliverance from slavery in Egypt. In round numbers, if the city of Jerusalem swelled with 100,000–150,000 pilgrims coming to celebrate, and if one lamb were sacrificed for every ten people, the blood of 10,000–15,000 lambs totaling hundreds of gallons was emptied out of one vessel after the next, washing over the base of the altar, swishing across the temple floor. Simultaneously, entrails were burned on the altar. The temple resembled a slaughterhouse. And so it had to happen to Jesus. Thousands of sacrificed animals and buckets of blood annually for centuries were leading up to nothing? No. The Christ, the Lamb of God, came to be slaughtered. He came for His blood to be poured out in order to be our sacrifice, to give us His true body and true blood in the holy Supper for forgiveness, for eternal life.

IN THE BODY AND THE BLOOD: NO MERE HISTORICAL FIGURE

If the body and blood of Christ our God, slaughtered for us on Good Friday, are not truly present at the Lord's Table, then our Savior would have been a mere historical figure, a distant memory of the Church, further removed with each passing generation (Sasse, 121). If Jesus does not speak a living, active Word, and if He is not giving to us His very body and blood, then what Gospel, what sure hope and comfort can there be? What good is a $10 million inheritance if it remains inaccessible under lock at the National Bank of Italy? But if the inheritance was deposited in increments of $100,000 into your bank account each month, that would make a $1.2 million annual difference for you. The *real presence* of the gift is what you need. There can be no Gospel, no comfort, without the Real Presence. *The body and blood* is not figurative language; it is the particular language of Jesus' own testament of what He did then and is doing now, for us and for our salvation. Two thousand years ago, God established the value of what Christ did for you at the cross and the tomb, and He sustains the benefit now with His Word and Sacrament: *take, eat . . . take, drink.* There deposited, with and under the bread and wine, *in the body and the blood,* God gives to you full forgiveness and a pledge, a guarantee, of your full inheritance of the paradise to come.

IN THE BODY AND THE BLOOD: JESUS' PROMISE TO EAT IN PARADISE

In the body and the blood, He will give to all the faithful His own self for heav'nly food. Heavenly food—to shore up our faith, to strengthen our love, to bestow forgiveness. It is so amazing that He would do this for us, give us so much through common bread and a sip of wine, by His Word's power. And the day will come for us when the sacramental meal gives way to the full banquet. In the Divine Service, we hear about the night when He was betrayed, when He took the bread, broke it, and gave it to disciples, and then the wine, proclaiming it is the blood of the new covenant. The Gospel of Matthew records something beautiful. Look closely at the second half of the verse. Jesus said:

> I will not drink again of this fruit of the vine until that day when I drink it new with you in My Father's kingdom. (Matthew 26:29)

"When I drink it new with you," Jesus promised. He will welcome us there. It is true—to Christians who gather with Jesus at His Table now, He assures a place at His Table upon His return.

> 3 Rank on rank the host of heaven
> Spreads its vanguard on the way
> As the Light of Light, descending
> From the realms of endless day,
> Comes the pow'rs of hell to vanquish
> As the darkness clears away.

Rank on Rank the Host of Heaven

God had His heavenly host, the angelic armies, ready to defend His Son that first Christmas because Satan was ready to attack. Disguised in the flesh of Herod, the evil one determined to destroy the Son through the command to kill the Bethlehem boys, and he would have succeeded had God not prophetically arranged for the baby's escape to Egypt.

Rank on rank the host of heaven reminds us that we must not reduce Christmas to sentimental feelings. Christmas Day marks the unfolding of the satanic battle against God's action for our salvation. God protected His Son at His birthplace to ensure His arrival at another town thirty-three years later, where the scourge and cross lay waiting. The calming scene *The little Lord Jesus asleep on the hay* in the beloved carol "Away in a Manger" (*LSB* 364:1) would not last.

Think of it this way: The birth of the One who is preceded by ranks of angels marks the point in time when God changed His dwelling place, the location of His holiness, from the stone temple in Jerusalem to the temple of His own flesh and blood. Jesus proclaimed, "Destroy this temple, and in three days I will raise it up" (John 2:19). From the place where His holiness and glory dwelt, between the cherubim of gold atop the ark of the covenant in the Most Holy Place, God would not conquer the powers of hell. Thousands of goats and lambs sacrificed throughout centuries culminate in the meaning and purpose of Christmas, when God renders obsolete the Jerusalem temple, becomes man, dwells among us, and conquers hell for us by arriving at the altar of the cross.

> Since therefore the children share in flesh and
> blood, He Himself likewise partook of the same
> things, that through death He might destroy the
> one who has the power of death, that is, the devil,
> and deliver all those who through fear of death
> were subject to lifelong slavery. (Hebrews 2:14–15)

Christmas means that the angels sing two messages—one regarding heaven and one regarding earth—for the same reason. The Son is born to endure the shame of the cross. It is the only way the pow'rs of hell to vanquish. It is the sole reason for glory to God in heaven and for peace on earth between God and those upon whom His favor rests (Just, *Luke 1:1–9:50*, 111).

This third stanza may point also to the ranks of angels preceding the Lord at His second coming in triumph, in full glory, with all power from above, with all the angels, for the final undoing of Satan, sin, death, and hell. Jesus promised multiple times, including when He encouraged His disciples not to be afraid to take up their cross and follow Him, that "the Son of Man is going to come with His angels in the glory of His Father" (Matthew 16:27).

From our vantage point, the birth of Christ with shepherds, angels, and a manger and the return of Christ in full glory with all authority, all angels, and all power appear as two different culminations in God's plan of salvation. Not so for the Creator. We all know the Bible verse, even if we do not recall that it was Peter who wrote it, that the Lord's return is certain: "But do not overlook this one fact, beloved, that with the Lord one day is as a thousand years, and a thousand years as one day. . . . The day of the Lord will come" (2 Peter 3:8, 10). We also know that the day has been set (Acts 17:31). A multitude of the heavenly host of angels (Luke 2:13) appeared to the shepherds; the ranks of angels will usher in His return. The battle that was begun in humility at Christmas reached its apex when the Son, in humiliating degradation, was nailed down a few feet above ground and cast a shadow of helpless defeat. But that changed. What appeared as defeat is revealed as victory at dawn three days later. The nails of death give way to scars of triumph. On the Last Day, Jesus will seal and proclaim the victory in full glory.

Now, with His true body and blood, He feeds, forgives, and preserves you. And then, the moment you see the ranks of angels usher Him in, He will welcome you to dine with Him at the feast that has no end. He assures you that your faith is not in vain; the One who came *from the realms of endless day* will call you to live and reign with Him there.

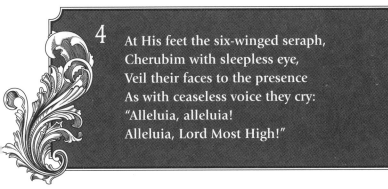

4 At His feet the six-winged seraph,
Cherubim with sleepless eye,
Veil their faces to the presence
As with ceaseless voice they cry:
"Alleluia, alleluia!
Alleluia, Lord Most High!"

Six-Winged Seraph,
Cherubim with Sleepless Eye

Isaiah saw them the year King Uzziah died. He saw the Lord in the temple, His massive train and six-winged seraphim flying, crying out: "Holy, holy, holy is the LORD of hosts; the whole earth is full of His glory!" (Isaiah 6:3). God's voice shook the foundations. Isaiah feared, "Woe is me!" (6:5). He knew that a sinner could not survive God's holiness. The Lord had mercy on him.

John the evangelist saw them too. "I looked, and behold, a door standing open in heaven!" (Revelation 4:1). A voice like a trumpet commanded, "Come up here" (4:1). John leaves the earth and enters. He sees Yahweh, whose glory and majesty are as brilliant as the bright sun shining through precious gemstones. John sees seraphim, as did Isaiah, with six wings "full of eyes all around" (Revelation 4:8), and day and night, *with sleepless eye*, "they never cease to say, 'Holy, holy, holy, is the Lord God Almighty'" (4:8).

Can we, in faith by His grace, at least acknowledge this—there is much more going on than we imagine. Winged creatures full of eyes? John and Isaiah hear them sing a hymn of praise. Down on earth, cherubim fashioned from gold were placed at each end of the ark of the covenant. There God promised to meet and speak with Moses (Exodus 25:22). Yahweh is enthroned on the cherubim, according to 1 Samuel 4:4 and 2 Samuel 6:2. The hymn, together with faith's eye, brings us to the throne room of heaven. The melody, beautiful, mysterious, and meditative, swells in each stanza, and we anticipate joining John and Isaiah and the winged creatures there before the Lord, with the twenty-four elders and "with all the company of heaven," singing our alleluias even as we now receive His very body and blood. *Alleluia!*

Please read Revelation 19:1–8. *Alleluia,* or *hallelujah,* means "Praise Yah," "Yah" being a short form of "Yahweh." *Alleluia,* "Praise Yah," is used four times in the entire New Testament, only in Revelation 19. We will look at the first three (Brighton, 485; see also 487–90).

> After this I heard what seemed to be the loud voice of a great multitude in heaven, crying out, "Hallelujah! Salvation and glory and power belong to our God." (Revelation 19:1)

Why do we praise great athletes? Why does a stadium erupt with roaring cheers? It is because the star has completed a stunning play to help the home team. No one cheers for a player who underperforms. By definition, whoever is God is deserving of and could, by authoritative right, demand praise and obedience. Marduk did. Allah does. But Yahweh is different. He comes to deliver. He comes to rescue and to save. Earthly performers and other so-called gods take your praise and pocketbook, even when providing nothing to cheer about. John, however, hears an immense crowd cheering, giving praise with a loud voice because God has judged as guilty the great prostitute who corrupted the earth with her immorality and murdered His servants (Revelation 19:2). *Alleluia!* She is locked away for all eternity, unable and never again to harm or threaten or tempt God's people.

> Once more they cried out, "Hallelujah!"
> The smoke from her goes up forever and ever.
> (Revelation 19:3)

Like driving up to a building that had been burned to the ground, smoldering, charred, black, and ruined, so too for the wicked prostitute—the judgment and punishment are permanent. It will never end. There is the might of God's salvation and glory and power for His people—He casts upon the satanic forces their due, incinerating those powers by abandoning His own Son, the Lamb of God, at the cross and driving Him into the fires of hell. Now in Revelation, John sees just condemnation, as the likes of the evil one is captured and "thrown alive into the lake of fire that burns with sulfur" (19:20). *Alleluia!*

> And the twenty-four elders and the four living creatures fell down and worshiped God who was seated on the throne, saying, "Amen. Hallelujah!" And from the throne came a voice saying, "Praise our God, all you His servants, you who fear Him, small and great." (Revelation 19:4–5)

Small and great, all are ushered in, welcomed to worship the One who sits on the throne and the Lamb. It is so wonderful to see a little word in verse 5, *small*. Does it need explaining? Great ones such as John the Baptist, courageous, beheaded, come to mind. And the six-winged creatures, the holy seraphim, with two wings covering their faces, unfit to be seen by or to look upon the One who sits enthroned. There is to be a place for me seated among the great as well. I am thankful for the word *small*, for God welcomes all, the small, even the sinful. The music intensifies— the congregation sings: *Alleluia, alleluia! Alleluia, Lord Most High!*

O Christ, Who Shared Our Mortal Life

1 O Christ, who shared our mortal life
And ended death's long reign,
Who healed the sick and raised the dead
And bore our grief and pain:
We know our years on earth are few,
That death is always near.
Come now to us, O Lord of Life;
Bring hope that conquers fear!

Raising of Jairus's Daughter (Matthew 9:18–19,
23–26 or Mark 5:21–43)

5 A ruler proud but bent by grief
Knelt down before Your feet:
"My precious daughter's gripped by death!
Come now and death defeat!"
A multitude had gathered round
To hear the truth You taught,
But, leaving them, You turned to help
A father sore distraught.

6 You pressed through crowds to reach the child
Whose limbs with death grew cold.
"She is not dead; she only sleeps!"
The weeping folk You told.
And then You took her hand and called,
"My child, I bid you rise!"
She rose! And all stood round You, Lord,
With awed and wond'ring eyes!

Raising of the Widow's Son (Luke 7:11–17)

7 The ranks of death with trophy grim
Through ancient streets once trod
And suddenly confronted You,
The mighty Son of God.
A widow's tears evoked Your Word;
You stopped the bearers' tread.
"Weep not!" in pity then You spoke
To her whose son was dead.

8 The ranks of death, the Lord of Life
Stood face to face that hour;
And You took up the age-old strife
With words of awesome pow'r.
"Young man, arise!" You ordered loud,
And death defeated lay.
The widow's son cast off his shroud
And strode from death away.

Raising of Lazarus (John 11:1–45)

9 Two weeping sisters, worn by grief
And mired in depths of gloom,
Stood watching where their brother lay
Within a rock-sealed tomb.
When, Lord, You met them as they mourned,
You wept compassion's tear.
But Martha, sore with sorrow, said,
"He'd lived had You been here!"

10 "I am the Lord of life and death!"
You answered Martha's cry,
"And all who hear and trust My Word
Shall live, although they die!"
You walked the path to Laz'rus' tomb,
You called him forth by name,
And living, loving once again,
From death to life he came!

4 Death's power holds us still in thrall
And bears us toward the tomb.
Death's dark'ning cloud hangs like a pall
That threatens earth with doom.
But You have broken death's embrace
And torn away its sting.
Restore to life our mortal race!
Raise us, O Risen King!

LSB 552
TEXT: HERMAN G. STUEMPFLE JR. (1923–2007), ALT.;
COPYRIGHT © 2006 GIA PUBLICATIONS, INC.

t first glance, this hymn appears to be a proclamation of God's power over death, as evidenced by the inclusion of the New Testament's accounts of the three people Jesus raised back to life: Jairus's daughter, the widow's son, and Lazarus. Actually, the entire hymn is a prayer, and those miracles are the hymn's impetus for petitioning the Lord to raise *us* from the dead. The first and last stanzas frame the inner stanzas, which proclaim Jesus' power over death. In the first stanza, we pray to the Lord *who shared our mortal life And ended death's long reign*, and in the last, we call upon Him to *raise us*.

Two phrases in particular, one from the first and one from the last stanza, form a sharp contrast of two truths that accentuate the hymn's outline. The stark reality confessed in the first stanza,

> *We know our years on earth are few, That death is*
> *always near*

is undone and overcome by the magnificent truth proclaimed in the last stanza:

> *But You have broken death's embrace And torn away*
> *its sting.*

Although death is close by, Christ has conquered it, releasing us from its grasp. The second words in each line—*know* and *You*—are key. What the author emphasizes with a crisp, two-part outline, the composer accentuates with a strong melody. The musical line corresponding to those two words calls us to attention. The opening interval is decisive. It reaches for and lands on the song's high note and holds it for an extra half-count to reinforce *know* and *You* and to amplify the truths mentioned above.

The skills of the author and composer add to the hymn's appeal and helpfulness. Most of all, the subject matter makes the hymn powerful. Can you think of anything more painful for a parent than to lose a child? Stand next to a mother in a hospital waiting room whose daughter is in surgery after a car accident. What comes from her the moment the surgeon steps through the doorway to say, "I am so sorry . . . " is unforgettable. Her immediate cry, more like a shriek, and nearby, her husband's buckling down, gives clues. Such immeasurable pain is given to few.

With this hymn, we praise and pray. We praise Jesus, reliving miracles, telling Him what He did, talking to Him, describing His miraculous action—*You turned to help . . . You took her hand and called; You stopped the bearers' tread . . . "Young man, arise!" You ordered loud. You answered Martha's cry . . . You called him forth by name.* The telling, the reliving of the miracles in our hearts as if we, too, were witnessing the events, tightens faith. Who speaks to death? Does death listen? Death likes being the boss. Death gives orders and stops life. It steals time, leaves memories, and forbids new ones. Nobody raises the dead, except Jesus. And He did. He raised to life three people. Recounting Jesus' miracles deepens our faith and moves us to pray with confidence because the One who raised the dead and who Himself was resurrected never to die again will raise us all.

When the hymn was first published, it spoke of the miracle of Jesus raising the widow's son, but not the other two. Our Commission on Worship approached the author, thinking how helpful it would be to include this hymn in *Lutheran Service Book*, particularly if he would write additional stanzas to address the raising of the synagogue ruler's daughter and the raising of Lazarus. Pastors would then have the option to select this hymn and employ the stanzas for the miracle that is recounted in the Gospel for the day.

"I am intrigued by the invitation," the author replied. "However, I have some other deadlines to meet, and we have a few family functions to attend. I may not be able to honor your request." It did not sound promising. To the surprise and delight of the committee, four new stanzas arrived in five days, two for each of the other two miracles. Each of the three accounts of Jesus' raising the dead was now accounted for in one hymn.

The author's style is captivating, not archaic. It causes one to keep reading. His artistry is colorful, lively, and easy to understand. His use of language helps build our trust in the Lord's work, His power over death, and His willingness and ability to intervene in our lives. With the inner stanzas we praise Jesus, retelling the biblical accounts of His restoring three people to earthly life. Singing those true stories gives praise to the Lord; brings the hearer of God's Word to the edge of Jesus' greater miracle, His own resurrection; and leads us to anticipate our triumph in Him. On the Last Day, all who are in the tombs will hear His voice and come out (John 5:28–29); by His sheer mercy, we will be raised imperishable (1 Corinthians 15:52) and will live with Him eternally.

> 1   O Christ, who shared our mortal life
> And ended death's long reign,
> Who healed the sick and raised the dead
> And bore our grief and pain:
> We know our years on earth are few,
> That death is always near.
> Come now to us, O Lord of Life;
> Bring hope that conquers fear!

Christ Shared Our Mortal Life

The prayer opens by identifying Jesus as the one *who shared our mortal life*. By itself, that provides zero comfort for those wise enough to admit the obvious—*We know our years on earth are few, That death is always near.* This is a problem. Everyone knows it. This is part of the reason why life's diversions are such an easy sale. We attempt to deflect from that fact, yet the fact remains. We have few years on earth. God reminds us—our days are like grass (Psalm 103:15) or a passing shadow (144:4). James says, "You are a mist that appears for a little time and then vanishes" (4:14). Solomon urges, "Do not boast about tomorrow, for you do not know what a day may bring" (Proverbs 27:1). And Moses knows that our years are "soon gone" and prays, "Teach us to number our days that we may get a heart of wisdom" (Psalm 90:10, 12).

We need the life of the One *who shared our mortal life* to stand apart from all others. Why? Moses knew to ask, "Who considers the power of Your anger?" (90:11). The big problem is not that death shortens life. The problem is that death brings us to God's wrath. His righteous anger relegates the sinful to hell. That's the problem. Hope comes not merely from His *sharing* our mortal life. It comes because of what He *accomplished with* His life, culminating in His ending death's long reign and including the destruction of death's underlying power—sin.

To accomplish this, to end the reign of death, Jesus worked out the progression noted by this hymn's author. First, He healed the sick, which is especially meaningful to those whose names are on their congregation's prayer list. For months we have been praying for a young mother whose grandparents belong to our parish. She would not end the life of her unborn baby boy after she and her husband were informed that carrying the baby to term would drastically decrease her chance of surviving cancer. The baby is baptized, happy, healthy, and will one day learn of her mother's love, who is receiving experimental treatment and for whom we still pray. Jesus healed many people with various diseases, and they rejoiced (Matthew 15:30–31). He did not and does not heal all.

Healing the sick, however, is His first step in His progression to end death's long reign. Sickness leads to death; therefore, it must be overcome. When death would strike before He would arrive, healing was no longer an option. He would do more. He raised the three people spoken of in the hymn—a synagogue ruler's little girl, a widow's only son, and his dear friend Lazarus, a brother of two sisters. Raising the dead—was it as unthinkable then as today? It was a remarkable, huge step in His progression toward ending the reign of death. It could not be the last step. He must do more because death, like sickness, stems from sin. In order to end the reign of sickness and death, Jesus must strike the root cause of both—the sinfulness that dwells within us. Our Lord's sacrifice and His mercy impart both the physical healing of sickness and death and the spiritual healing of sin. Scripture often pairs the two (Psalm 103:2–3; Matthew 8:16–17; 9:2–8, for example), and this is especially so according to Isaiah, whose string of phrases describing the work of the Savior merges physical and spiritual healing. Ultimately, eliminating sin removes sickness and death. Permanently healing sickness and overcoming death are not done without overcoming sin. "Surely He has borne our griefs and carried our sorrows. . . . He was pierced for our transgressions;

He was crushed for our iniquities; . . . with His wounds we are healed" (Isaiah 53:4-5).

Because the One *who shared our mortal life* healed the sick, raised the dead, and bore our grief and pain, we can admit, while holding on to the hope that conquers fear, that *We know our years on earth are few, That death is always near.* We pray for healing. We continue to pray for the young mother and others like her, knowing that if sickness leads to death, our trust is in the Lord of Life, who has destroyed it all—sickness, death, and sin. We pray to Him, *Come now.*

Let us turn now to the miracles of Jesus that move us to praise Him and to trust Him—His raising to life the synagogue ruler's daughter; His raising to life the widow's son; His raising to life Lazarus. I am grateful to our seminary professors Dr. Voelz, Dr. Gibbs, and Dr. Just for providing keen insights on these biblical accounts in their respective commentaries (*Mark 1:1–8:26* [370-75], *Matthew 1:1–11:1* [483-85], *Luke 1:1–9:50* [307-10]).

5 A ruler proud but bent by grief
Knelt down before Your feet:
"My precious daughter's gripped by death!
Come now and death defeat!"
A multitude had gathered round
To hear the truth You taught,
But, leaving them, You turned to help
A father sore distraught.

6 You pressed through crowds to reach the child
Whose limbs with death grew cold.
"She is not dead; she only sleeps!"
The weeping folk You told.
And then You took her hand and called,
"My child, I bid you rise!"
She rose! And all stood round You, Lord,
With awed and wond'ring eyes!

A Father Sore Distraught

Jesus intervenes in a powerful man's life to restore his daughter to life. The story is personal and real. The beautiful writing of the hymn's author with the composer's bold melody help carry the account into our hearts. The word order accents the opening line. Typically, we would say "a proud ruler." Hearing instead *a ruler proud* swings the emphasis to the adjective and sets up the contrast with the next short phrase. He is *bent by grief*. A father's pride will not hold when his daughter lies dying. Success is no match for death, not when it threatens your little girl.

Mark's Greek (5:22) indicates that the synagogue ruler does not kneel. He prostrates himself. With a signal of desperation, faith, and need, he falls to the ground, all the way down, at Jesus' feet. His daughter is *gripped by death*! He can do nothing. He has nothing to offer to the One who controls everything. He pleads that Jesus come lay His hands on her so she may be—and then most interestingly, the ruler does not use the Greek word for *healed*. He uses the Greek word for *saved* (Voelz, 373). Why? In context, *saved* includes physical healing and more. The man of faith lying facedown before God knows what he needs. Perhaps the Lord would not heal his daughter to spare her life, so he would plead with Him to save her from eternal death. While Jesus was healing the woman who had a discharge of blood (Mark 5:24–34), the synagogue ruler's daughter died. Jesus goes to the man's house, to the little girl *whose limbs with death grew cold.* Have you ever placed your hand on the hand or arm of a loved one whose body is in the casket? Never mind how nicely the undertaker has applied the makeup, the cold limb tells the truth. What happens next—Jesus touching the dead girl, taking her by the hand, commanding as if she can hear, "Little girl, arise!" and raising her to life—astounded all, and is linked to a remarkable aspect of Christian faith. The concept stems from Jesus' own words: "The kingdom of heaven is at hand" (Matthew 3:2; 4:17; Mark 1:15). What did Jesus mean by "the kingdom of heaven"? What actually was happening when Jesus healed the sick, blind, deaf, paralyzed, and even the dead?

Yes, the miracles were life-changing events flowing from Jesus' compassion. Imagine the joy of the father! But there is more to it. When Jesus is present, the kingdom of God is at hand, meaning not a geographic location but His reigning, end-times power (Gibbs, *Matthew 1:1–11:1,* 49). When Jesus walked through Galilee, He brought with Him the features and likenesses of the age to come, the essence of paradise, of His eternal, reigning will, giving to us a preview of what will be. When Jesus returns, when He unfolds for us the new and perfect age, there can be no sick, demon-possessed, blind, paralyzed, or dead. Said liturgically in a Post-Communion Collect, Jesus brings "a foretaste of the feast to come" (*LSB*, p. 166). He brings a preview, but not a complete view. Jesus unfolds a portion of the blessings of the age to come *ahead of time.*

For now, the signs of the present age remain. Jesus did not heal everyone. He did not restore every dead child to physical life. Nevertheless, He broke into our world, which was ruled by death, and ushered in His reigning power—the age to come, ahead of time (Matthew 8:29), as if to say, "Behold the power of God. See now what is still to come!" The little girl's restoration points to the Lord's resurrection and reveals the unfolding of God's eternal peace upon His return, when "He will raise me and all the dead, and give eternal life to me and all believers in Christ" (Small Catechism, explanation of the Third Article).

7
The ranks of death with trophy grim
Through ancient streets once trod
And suddenly confronted You,
The mighty Son of God.
A widow's tears evoked Your Word;
You stopped the bearers' tread.
"Weep not!" in pity then You spoke
To her whose son was dead.

8
The ranks of death, the Lord of Life
Stood face to face that hour;
And You took up the age-old strife
With words of awesome pow'r.
"Young man, arise!" You ordered loud,
And death defeated lay.
The widow's son cast off his shroud
And strode from death away.

The Ranks of Death

Who are the ranks, and what is the trophy? "A considerable crowd," Luke reports (7:12), fills the ranks of death. Probably most of us, if not all, have participated in a procession to the grave site, to the squared hole in the ground where the bright green fake-grass mat covering the dirt pile softens our senses to what is about to happen. Some years ago, my childhood best friend and his wife could not have known that they were about to lead the procession. House sold, all packed, ready to move across country, their sixteen-year-old son met up with a couple of friends for a simple ride. There was no alcohol, no reckless-ness. But instantly, my friend's family no longer numbered five. We processed with them, prayed, and with every other parent, wondered "What if it had been my son?" We heard a wonderful sermon. The boy's mother said, "I thought I wanted to hear about my son, but we heard about Christ. It is what I needed. Pastor said that it appears like death has stolen time, but knowing that because Christ is risen, that He has destroyed death and restores life—His peace is mine."

The *ranks of death* also infer the spiritual forces of evil (Ephesians 6:12), who are proud and happy to be leading the parade and who with death's *trophy grim*—the corpse!—*suddenly confronted You, The Mighty Son of God.* Death's spiritual forces are about to be turned back. Jesus touches the coffin and stops the procession. *The ranks of death, the Lord of Life Stood face to face that hour.* Jesus seems outnumbered. The ranks of death have walked the cemetery path hundreds, thousands of times. The hole always gets filled. Faith's imagination hears the snickering of the spiritual forces hovering above their *trophy grim.* Not this time, not when the mighty Son, manifesting the end-times power of God, puts His hand on the coffin. At the high point in the hymn's melody, we sing, *"Young man, arise!"* proclaiming to one another, praising the Lord, exclaiming, *You ordered loud, And death defeated lay.* And through the message of praise, the Lord of life emboldens our faith and moves us to pray.

"The dead man sat up and began to speak," Luke reports (Luke 7:15). If his sitting up left any in doubt, hearing him speak brought confirmation and no small amount of fear (7:15–16). The hymn's author describes the miracle's impact, *The widow's son cast off his shroud*, a clear reference to Isaiah's prophecy (25:7–8) that God will "swallow up . . . the covering that is cast over all peoples, the veil that is spread over all nations. He will swallow up death forever."

There is one more aspect to the story, common to the other times Jesus raised a dead person to life, that is missing. Recall that Jairus feared losing his daughter. He fell facedown at Jesus' feet "and implored Him earnestly, . . . 'Come and lay Your hands on her, so she may be made well'" (Mark 5:23). Regarding Lazarus, Mary and Martha sent word to Jesus, "Lord, he whom You love is ill" (John 11:3), meaning, "Please hurry! Have mercy! Heal him!"

In these two accounts, as with other healing miracles, someone cries to the Lord, and He answers. Not this time. Luke is not one to miss a detail, yet in this account he makes no mention of anyone's faith or anyone's request. The widow walks, cries, mourns, and Jesus is moved by her tears, but neither she nor anyone else has made a plea (Just, *Luke 1:1–9:50*, 308).

God loves to answer prayer. He does not always wait for it. Compassion does not always look for an invitation any more than a mother waits for her child to say, "I don't feel very good" before she brings love, medicine, and another blanket (Isaiah 49:15). It is our privilege to pray. Our Father listens. Sometimes He is moved to intervene in a manner He might not have if the plea had not been made. But our prayers are not the key that unlocks God's mercy. "When the Lord saw her, He had compassion on her" (Luke 7:13). Healing and forgiveness come because God is abounding in steadfast love. His compassion is coupled with divine power to change the direction of an otherwise normal, sure, and certain course of events. "Young man, arise!" *And death defeated lay.*

We have all the reason to praise and to pray. It is comforting to know that our God, by His grace, converts, guards, forgives, and keeps us, and He will raise us. He surely will, for He is the one whose infinite compassion gave up His Son to make it so.

9   Two weeping sisters, worn by grief
     And mired in depths of gloom,
     Stood watching where their brother lay
     Within a rock-sealed tomb.
     When, Lord, You met them as they mourned,
     You wept compassion's tear.
     But Martha, sore with sorrow, said,
     "He'd lived had You been here!"

10   "I am the Lord of life and death!"
     You answered Martha's cry,
     "And all who hear and trust My Word
     Shall live, although they die!"
     You walked the path to Laz'rus' tomb,
     You called him forth by name,
     And living, loving once again,
     From death to life he came!

From Death to Life He Came!

Everyone at the scene believes it is the final detail. Lazarus *lay within a rock-sealed tomb.* In Luke 7, we hear that Jesus raised the widow's son without her having asked. Perhaps she did not even know Him. But Mary and Martha know Jesus, and they asked. Jesus loves them, and He loves their brother, Lazarus (John 11:5). Their friendship is deep. But after hearing of Lazarus's illness, Jesus stayed away from him two more days. Martha was *sore with sorrow.* Sore? Does the author mean upset at Jesus, even angry? I might have been. *He'd lived had You been here!* Perhaps you have had your own grief and do not need to imagine the sisters' grief and disappointment.

Jesus responds: "Lazarus has died, and for your sake I am glad that I was not there" (11:14–15), a revelation about the kind of love that kept Him from going immediately to Lazarus. What kind of love? Jesus explains, "I am glad that I was not there, *so that you may believe*" (v. 15, emphasis added). His reason for delaying to come makes sense for all who know how the story ends. In that moment, though, it did not make sense to the disciples or to Lazarus's sisters. Christians today know that Jesus had much more in store for the siblings than they could comprehend. This is how we can know that the same is true for us, especially when life's circumstances tempt us to doubt whether Jesus is near, cares, or is in control. Jesus' love is not nearsighted. He will heal sick people, raise dead people, and much more. He will come forth from His own tomb in order to raise us to live with Him in the new creation.

> *And all who hear and trust My Word*
> *Shall live, although they die!*

Jesus said, "So that you may believe" (11:15). But no one decides to have faith, any more than Lazarus decided to come to life again. Sure, humanly speaking, psychologically speaking, every day around the world, it appears as though new adult converts have made a decision to have faith in Christ. The reality is that the Holy Spirit has been at work with the Word—read, taught, preached, shared, studied—to create living faith in the new believer's formerly dead heart. If the believer is responsible for igniting faith in his own heart after first checking the evidence, then why did only some of the Jews believe in Jesus after witnessing Lazarus walking out of the tomb? If you had known Lazarus, knew he was dead four days, saw him come out, saw others take off the grave wrappings, wouldn't you conclude that the One who did this has the power of God? The miracle is so astounding, what other explanation is there for the fact that many Jews believed, while others did not. Instead, they "went to the Pharisees and told them what Jesus had done" (11:46), not as an act of praise, but to tattle and, in fact, their reporting led the council and Caiaphas to plot to kill Him (11:47–53). Again, to see and not to believe gives evidence to what Scripture says is true. Spiritually, our hearts are stone-cold dead from birth.

Therefore, we can pray, "Dear Lord, thank You for using Your life-giving Word to raise Lazarus from the dead and to create faith in me, who was spiritually dead—unable to fear, love, and trust in You. Thank You that I do not have to rely on the weakness of my own decisions and convictions for my salvation. Rather, I rely on Your mercy and the strength of Your grace for having acted on my spiritually dead heart. Amen."

Why did Jesus need to tell them, "Unbind him, and let him go" (John 11:44)? Martha believed that Jesus is the Christ (11:27), but she did not expect Jesus to raise Lazarus. "Lord, by this time there will be an odor, for he has been dead four days" (11:39). No one contradicted her: "Martha, just wait! Jesus is about to raise him up!" No one expected Jesus to call into the tomb or to see four-days-dead Lazarus walk out. Had you been standing a stone's throw away, watching with the others, would your jaw not have dropped? Maybe with a hint of joy, Jesus told them what to do, as if to say, "How long are you going to stand and stare? Untangle him!"

Jesus' mercy and display of power to undo death—*within a rock-sealed tomb*—pulls our eyes to the tomb Jesus left empty on the third day, substantiating John's claim, "Jesus loved Martha and her sister and Lazarus" (11:5), and Jesus' own testimony, "I am the resurrection and the life. Whoever believes in Me, though he die, yet shall he live, and everyone who lives and believes in Me shall never die" (11:25–26).

> 4   Death's power holds us still in thrall
> And bears us toward the tomb.
> Death's dark'ning cloud hangs like a pall
> That threatens earth with doom.
> But You have broken death's embrace
> And torn away its sting.
> Restore to life our mortal race!
> Raise us, O Risen King!

Death's Power Holds Us Still in Thrall

No, not enthralled—*in thrall*, a state of being controlled or captive. Death's power, its thrall, controls and dominates. It does not delight. It definitely does not let go. Imagine death's power holding you with the strength of a winch and half-inch-thick cable with a two-ton-load capacity. Death has the cable wrapped around your waist, snug, tight, and the winch switch is flipped on—feel the pull. You cannot outmuscle the winch, and you surely cannot break the cable. Live, marry, work, help, rest, travel, and what is left at the end of each day? Less cable, for *Death's power . . . bears us toward the tomb.*

The hymn's author compares death to a dark cloud hanging over *like a pall.* Even if you don't live in tornado alley, you know what eerily dark storm clouds look like. These illustrations are helpful—cables, clouds, palls—but completely unnecessary when death is so close you can see it coming, when a gray complexion is reflected in the mirror or the oxygen tank follows you or the hospice nurse is near.

Because we are not strong or faithful enough, we bend and break things we never intended to—vows, promises, and hearts. Scripture calls this activity sin. The consequence of sin—death's embrace—is something we cannot break. Death's embrace will not let go. Everyone knows it. Everyone coming out of Nain with the widow and her dead son knew it. No one expected him to sit up just because Jesus stopped the processional (Luke 7:11–17). In the home of the synagogue ruler, when Jesus prepared to raise the little girl, the people laughed (Mark 5:38–40). The world laughs in the face of Christians every time we confess, "I believe in . . . the forgiveness of sins, the resurrection of the body, and the life everlasting" (Apostles' Creed). Yet we believe it, and we sing one of the most powerful phrases of the hymn with the melody's highest note assigned to the second word: *But You have broken death's embrace And torn away its sting.*

When death approaches and misses, when the life of a child is spared or chemo wipes out the cancer, we are so thankful. One family's little boy from our church was diagnosed with leukemia. His parents prayed, awake all night, waiting in fear to learn whether their son's cancer was curable. They appreciate the story of Jairus. When the Lord spares life, as He did for the boy with leukemia, or restores life, as He did in the case of the three families in the hymn, fear and deep sadness give way to astonishment and gladness. Through these acts of almighty compassion, the Lord points to the Last Day, when He will raise, physically, from death to everlasting life, all the baptized who lived and died in Christ.

The sting of death is not the shortening of life and the sadness surrounding it. The sting of death is sin because of the power of the Law, which accuses us before God in the moment of death. Guilty sinners deserve damnation. But by His crucifixion, Jesus took death's sting, absorbing into Himself the due punishment for our sin. By His resurrection, He stands triumphant over sin and death. It is so amazing.

The hymn's author concludes where he began, in prayer to Christ, who came into this world to share our mortal life, drawing attention once more to our mortality, to our inability, and therefore to our total, complete dependency upon Him to rescue us. The One who kept His promise, "Destroy this temple, and in three days I will raise it up" (John 2:19) and who is the Creator of all things "visible and invisible" (Colossians 1:16) is the One who has *broken death's embrace* and who will *restore to life our mortal race!*

O Come, O Come, Emmanuel

1   O come, O come, Emmanuel,
    And ransom captive Israel,
    That mourns in lonely exile here
    Until the Son of God appear.

Refrain
    Rejoice! Rejoice! Emmanuel
    Shall come to thee, O Israel!

2   O come, Thou Wisdom from on high,
    Who ord'rest all things mightily;
    To us the path of knowledge show,
    And teach us in her ways to go.
        Refrain

3   O come, O come, Thou Lord of might,
    Who to Thy tribes on Sinai's height
    In ancient times didst give the Law
    In cloud and majesty and awe.
        Refrain

4 O come, Thou Branch of Jesse's tree,
    Free them from Satan's tyranny
    That trust Thy mighty pow'r to save,
    And give them vict'ry o'er the grave.
        Refrain

5 O come, Thou Key of David, come,
    And open wide our heav'nly home;
    Make safe the way that leads on high,
    And close the path to misery.
        Refrain

6 O come, Thou Dayspring from on high,
    And cheer us by Thy drawing nigh;
    Disperse the gloomy clouds of night,
    And death's dark shadows put to flight.
        Refrain

7 O come, Desire of nations, bind
    In one the hearts of all mankind;
    Bid Thou our sad divisions cease,
    And be Thyself our King of Peace.
        Refrain

LSB 357
TEXT: LATIN, C. TWELFTH CENTURY
TRANSLATION: JOHN MASON NEALE (1818–66), ALT.

dvent is a preparatory time for Christmas joy, for Jesus' arrival and incarnation. We know this. Advent also emphasizes our anticipation of the unending joy that is ours when our Lord returns. We know this too. And of course throughout Advent, as on any given day, we rejoice in knowing that God comes to us in His Word, the Supper, and Baptism. Many pastors have a concern however. If today's brisk economy and twenty-first-century lifestyles paired with technology of online shopping keep no one waiting or wanting for anything, does anyone need Advent? Or more to the point: does anyone need Christ?

We know, of course, that the capacity to fill life with entertainment is no substitute for Emmanuel. Neither is the tendency to minimize the seriousness of our pain, problems, and sin. Examples of this are everywhere. Marriage is not delightful for every couple. Many marriages thrive, and it is encouraging to see, although seeing how happy another couple is can also raise guilt or regret about one's own. For many, though, marriage has brought pain, extending to and through divorce. There are also folks, sadly, who attach false hope to marriage aberrations, including fornication, cohabitation, and homosexuality. In that regard, the issue for those of us not trapped in these particular sins is the fear of lovingly confronting someone who is.

Why raise such touchy issues in an introduction to an Advent hymn? Because people will match their denial of the seriousness of sin and pain with indifference to Christ's promise to return. We poke at touchy issues to help us see clearly. Whether it is because of excessive craving of pleasure, addiction to sin, or weakness in combating or confronting it, not to mention the daily threat of death, we need Emmanuel to come. We need the sure hope of Advent. This hymn is loved because it speaks of the hope that is ours in God's Son, in spite of any struggle or trouble.

The angel introduced to Mary her own season of Advent: "You will conceive in your womb. . . . You shall call His name Jesus" (Luke 1:31). Imagine her anticipation, accepting in faith that the baby she carries fulfills centuries-old divine promises, that the child is God's Son. Her relative Elizabeth, filled with the

Holy Spirit, identifies the child in Mary, exclaiming, "Blessed are you among women. . . . And why is this granted to me that the mother of my Lord should come to me?" (vv. 42–43). Mary herself is overcome and sings, "My soul magnifies the Lord, and my Spirit rejoices in God my Savior" (vv. 46–47).

Mary and Elizabeth teach us to embrace Advent. This season brings hope and welcomes honesty for Christians who understand both emotional pain and earthly joy and who are wise to know that neither has the last word. We can be straightforward about our troubles and not minimize them. We can enjoy hard work and life's pleasures without employing them as sedatives for life's pain. We do not need to minimize the seriousness of our sin and of God's judgment. Instead, we can be honest because God has given us strong faith to believe our hymn's refrain: *Rejoice! Rejoice! Emmanuel shall come to thee, O Israel!* We are God's chosen people, the new Israel, and our joyous hope is in the forgiveness of sins and His sure return.

Try to imagine what it would have been like to live in the eighth century, twelve hundred years ago. Did people wonder about the next famine or plague or freezing to death or if their baby would live or about the water supply? They had real concerns and confronted them with faith in Emmanuel. They knew about Advent. Their seasonal custom included a special focus during the seven evenings leading up to Christmas Eve. The evening worship service included Mary's song—her response to the angel and to Elizabeth—known to us as the Magnificat (Luke 1:46–55). The first line is cited above. These eighth-century Christians attached one of seven unique prayers each night to the beginning and end of the Magnificat. With each prayer, called an antiphon, God's people cried out to Jesus by addressing Him with an Old Testament title. The prayer described Jesus according to the title's meaning and then petitioned Him to come. In the eighth century, Christians in Advent called out to the Lord in prayer, knowing that as He kept His Word for Israel according to the angel Gabriel's announcement to Mary, He would keep His Word for them: *Rejoice! Rejoice! Emmanuel shall come to thee,*

O Israel! The One who came to rest in the manger will come again on the clouds of glory.

The hymn stanzas date to the twelfth century and are based on these eighth-century prayers of our ancestors. With the hymn, we sing them in order, except the prayer for December 23, the last prayer, has become the hymn's first stanza, with the name *Emmanuel* the basis for the refrain.

> *December 17*
>> O Wisdom,
>> proceeding from the mouth of the Most High,
>> pervading and permeating all creation,
>>> mightily ordering all things:
>> Come and teach us the way of prudence.

> *December 18*
>> O Adonai and ruler of the house of Israel,
>> who appeared to Moses in the burning bush
>>> and gave him the Law on Sinai:
>> Come with an outstretched arm and redeem us.

> *December 19*
>> O Root of Jesse,
>> standing as an ensign before the peoples,
>>> before whom all kings are mute, to whom the
>>> nations will do homage:
>> Come quickly to deliver us.

> *December 20*
>> O Key of David and scepter of the house
>>> of Israel,
>> You open and no one can close, You close and
>>> no one can open:
>> Come and rescue the prisoners who are in
>>> darkness and the shadow of death.

December 21

> O Dayspring,
> splendor of light everlasting:
> Come and enlighten those who sit in darkness
> and in the shadow of death.

December 22

> O King of the nations,
> the ruler they long for, the cornerstone
> uniting all people:
> Come and save us all, whom You formed
> out of clay.

December 23

> O Emmanuel,
> our king and our Lord, the anointed for the
> nations and their Savior:
> Come and save us, O Lord our God.

1   O come, O come, Emmanuel,
    And ransom captive Israel,
    That mourns in lonely exile here
    Until the Son of God appear.
    Refrain
    Rejoice! Rejoice! Emmanuel
    Shall come to thee, O Israel!

O Come, O Come, Emmanuel

*L*et us begin with the name for Jesus—*Emmanuel*—the name the evangelist uses by quoting Isaiah (Matthew 1:23). We all know what Emmanuel means—*God with us*—and the phrase is packed with meaning. If Jesus is *God with us*, then with Jesus comes all the Old Testament saving power of God. The God who promised Moses, who was afraid to approach Pharaoh, "I will be with you," and who assured him when he feared speaking, "Who has made man's mouth? . . . I will be with your mouth" (Exodus 3:12; 4:11–12), is the God who accomplished all the mighty works Moses reports in the first fifteen chapters of Exodus. *That* God is Emmanuel, *that* God is with us, and *that* God is Jesus.

Jesus is Emmanuel to "save His people from their sins" (Matthew 1:21). *Saving* includes *forgiving*. *Forgiveness* is the reason Jesus came to earth, to grant us redemption through His blood (Ephesians 1:7). But isn't it obvious? We are not only in *spiritual* bondage. Just as the Israelites were physically enslaved by Pharaoh unto death, so do death and illness and disease hold *us* physically captive. The impact of sin sweeps over us spiritually *and* physically. Jesus is Emmanuel who comes to save our souls *and* our bodies. Our greatest and ultimate hope is not "to die and go to heaven" as we often say. Our ultimate certain hope is for Emmanuel's return! In Advent, we prepare not only to rejoice in the *birth* of

Emmanuel, but we pray also for the *return* of Emmanuel, when Jesus will open up salvation for us, the new heavens and earth, the new Jerusalem, in all fullness and glory (Revelation 21:10–21).

Approximately thirty years ago, errant heart surgery for my nephew, a toddler, resulted in brain damage. He lost control of every voluntary muscle. Think about that. Medication and therapy reduced his symptoms somewhat. When he was little he would pray, "Dear Jesus, please take away my wiggles." I mean, try to teach your child to read when he cannot hold his head still. When he was a bit older he would pray, "Lord, please let the medicine and therapy work." Eventually he prayed, "Lord, please give me a miracle. Let me walk and talk in a normal way." No miracle came. He stopped asking, but God has kept his faith strong. A couple of weeks ago, Nancy and I made new friends at a wedding reception. Their third child was struck by an aggressive autistic strain. Now she is twelve years old. She cannot talk. These parents and their three other children love this girl deeply, and they learn from her unyielding love. They cherish Baptism, God's promise to connect her to Christ's death and resurrection, a little girl who, barring a miracle similar to the one our nephew prayed for, will live her life without ever singing a Christmas hymn or reciting the Apostles' Creed.

Even so, our friends enjoy God's gifts, being a family, serving others, and in keeping with trying circumstances, they sing with great longing: *O Come, O Come, Emmanuel.* My nephew accepts God's will and lives life energetically as best he is able with the love and close attention of his parents. They, too, live with heightened anticipation for Emmanuel to return and impart full relief and complete healing. Jesus was born physically, suffered physically, died physically, rose physically, appeared physically, and ascended physically not to save us only spiritually. He did not die to save our souls only, as if our bodies did not need saving, or as if they did not matter to Him. He did it all to deliver us from sin's complete hold—spiritual *and* physical. Therefore, we pray for the day when He completes the healing and restoration in the power of the resurrection.

Christians, from the Middle Ages to today, wherever there is physical suffering, disease, and death, are called together by the Spirit with the Word working in their hearts, and they know Advent's song. *O Come, O Come, Emmanuel, And ransom captive Israel.*

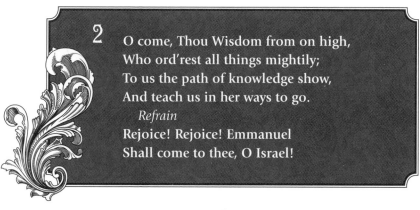

2   O come, Thou Wisdom from on high,
Who ord'rest all things mightily;
To us the path of knowledge show,
And teach us in her ways to go.
Refrain
Rejoice! Rejoice! Emmanuel
Shall come to thee, O Israel!

O Come, Thou Wisdom from on High

Wisdom is a person. More accurately, God's Son is called *Wisdom.* Solomon personifies wisdom in Proverbs 8. Wisdom, the Word, works with the Father in the creation of the universe and becomes human when He is conceived by the Spirit in the womb of Mary (Proverbs 8:22–31; John 1:3). He is the one *Who ord'rest all things mightily.* Teaching the Corinthians, emphasizing that he preaches "Christ crucified, a stumbling block to Jews and folly to Gentiles," the apostle Paul calls Christ "the power of God and the wisdom of God" (1 Corinthians 1:23–24) and says that in Him "are hidden all the treasures of wisdom and knowledge" (Colossians 2:3). Our Savior is called *Wisdom.* What is the wisdom we receive from Him, for which we pray *To us the path of knowledge show*? "The fear of the LORD is the beginning of wisdom" (Psalm 111:10). What does this mean?

On the one hand, I am wise to fear God's wrath whenever my sinful nature is directing traffic, telling me to turn away from what Wisdom says is pure, good, helpful, and unselfish. There are times when *fear* means fear! Sexual perversity, Solomon stresses, is a prime example of, even a symbol for, the exact opposite of wisdom. The adulteress with her seductive words knows what to say and how to dress in order to lure a young man to her bed of death (Proverbs 6:24–35; 7). Neither does wisdom have anything to do with being a quarrelsome wife (21:9) or a short-fused husband (14:29; 26:21) or a gossip (18:8). Wisdom values diligence and links laziness with shame (10:4–5). Wisdom cherishes honesty, justice, and kindness, while God warns that the self-righteous, proud, and arrogant will be destroyed (11:2; 16:18). On the other hand, for children of God who are filled with the Spirit of wisdom, and thus are grateful to Him for His sacrifice, to fear the Lord means to cling to the Lord in all things and to know that salvation is secure in Him.

Job 28 describes the efforts man will exert to find precious stones. Regardless what value people assign to rocks in the ground, what is the comparative value of wisdom in Christ? What do you attempt to mine from this world, believing it is of great worth, while often passing over the wisdom of Jesus? Jesus says that those who hunger and thirst for righteousness will be satisfied (Matthew 5:6) and those who hear and keep His Word are blessed (Luke 11:28). For Jeremiah, the Word was his heart's delight. He knew he was called by the name of the Lord, and so are you (Jeremiah 15:16). Isaiah wonders rhetorically why we spend, labor, and wrestle for what does not satisfy (55:2). The psalmist sings, "The law of the Lord is perfect, reviving the soul" (Psalm 19:7), the fear of the Lord is clean (19:9), and he desires the Word more than gold. The Word is sweeter than honey (19:10).

What is the value of stone, of *anything* we sweat over, compared to the value of Wisdom, which is to say, the value of God's Son? To fear the Lord is to know that He is "merciful and gracious, slow to anger, and abounding in steadfast love and faithfulness" (Exodus 34:6). To fear the Lord is to say with confidence, "The Lord is my helper; I will not fear; what can man do to me?" (Hebrews 13:6; Psalm 56:11; 118:6). To be free of all fears but one is Wisdom's gift to you. *Rejoice! Rejoice! Emmanuel shall come to thee, O Israel!*

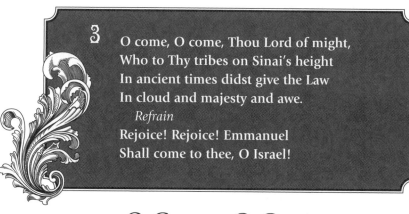

3 O come, O come, Thou Lord of might,
Who to Thy tribes on Sinai's height
In ancient times didst give the Law
In cloud and majesty and awe.
Refrain
Rejoice! Rejoice! Emmanuel
Shall come to thee, O Israel!

O Come, O Come, Thou Lord of Might

To better grasp how the refrain of this hymn is a promise of relief for those who have just sung of the Law, we put ourselves in the past and approach Mount Sinai with the Israelites of old.

We remember the night we crossed the sea, our fear as the Egyptians marched toward us (Exodus 14:10). We can still hear Moses promise, "Fear not, stand firm, and see the salvation of the LORD. . . . For the Egyptians whom you see today, you shall never see again" (v. 13). What happened then was inconceivable. Moses stretched out his hand over the sea, and the Lord drove the sea back with a strong wind all night. Then we went into the midst of the sea on dry ground, with a wall of water on each side! The Egyptians pursued, the Lord threw them into a panic, and they tried to flee. Then Moses, at the Lord's command, stretched out his arm once more, and the waters returned. We saw dead Egyptians strewn across the seashore (vv. 21–30). God saved us. He eliminated the Egyptian death threat. It was frightening. He caused our fear, love, and trust in Him to surge (vv. 30–31).

That was three months ago (Exodus 19:1). Now we are encamped in the Sinai wilderness before the mountain. Moses went up the mountain to God (v. 3), and the Lord told Moses to tell the people, "You yourselves have seen what I did to the Egyptians" (vv. 3-4).

When Moses told us, we recalled the gnats, flies, boils, and hail, all the plagues (Exodus 8-10), the screams of death from the houses of Egypt on Passover (12:29-30), and the host of us all, six hundred thousand men, with wives and children, flocks and herds, all on foot (vv. 37-38), with the Lord going before us, a pillar of cloud by day and a pillar of fire by night, and how He did not depart from us (13:21-22), all leading up to the sea crossing. We saw it all. We lived it.

Now Moses tells us that the Lord promises that we are His treasured possession among all peoples and that we are to keep His covenant. All together we said, "All that the LORD has spoken we will do" (19:5-8). On the morning of the third day, the mountain is consumed with thunder, lightning, a thick cloud, and a very loud trumpet blast. We trembled (v. 16). The mountain was wrapped in smoke because the Lord descended on it in fire. The mountain trembled. The trumpet grew louder. God called Moses to the top of the mountain (vv. 18-20).

Moses came down and told us the words God spoke: "I am the LORD your God, who brought you out of the land of Egypt, out of the house of slavery" (Exodus 20:1-2). The commandments He gives sound good, not like warnings, but like a commonsense description for the children He saved from Pharaoh to live in a loving, trusting relationship with Him and with one another. How could we possibly love and trust some other god? Did some other god part the sea? Why would we misuse His name and not call upon Him in the day of trouble? Surely we will pause each week to rest in His grace. We will honor our parents, for He chose them to give us life. We will protect life, marriage, one another's property and name, for we are created in His image to love and serve one another. We will love Him and one another, won't we (20:3-17)?

We surely desire to love Him and to serve others. However, it does not always go well. Sometimes we consciously disregard His Law. Or when we try to keep it, we often fail. Sometimes we attempt to prop ourselves up by looking down on others, or we dismiss the seriousness of our sin. What are we to do? We can thank God for His people of the Middle Ages and for the antiphon they wrote on which this stanza is based. They knew what to pray, recognizing the Lord almighty as the Lawgiver: "Come with an outstretched arm and redeem us." With an outstretched arm, the Lord delivered Israel out of Egypt. He did not stop there. He came to Bethlehem to deliver us from the Law's condemnation. Jesus is Emmanuel, God with us. *Rejoice! Rejoice! Emmanuel shall come to thee, O Israel!*

4   O come, Thou Branch of Jesse's tree,
     Free them from Satan's tyranny
     That trust Thy mighty pow'r to save,
     And give them vict'ry o'er the grave.
       Refrain
     Rejoice! Rejoice! Emmanuel
     Shall come to thee, O Israel!

O Come, Thou Branch of Jesse's Tree

The prophet calls the *Branch of Jesse's tree* "a shoot from the stump of Jesse" (Isaiah 11:1). Who is Jesse, why was he a stump, and what about the shoot? Jesse owned sheep. God chose Jesse's youngest son, David, a shepherd boy, to become a great king of Israel. God put His spirit upon David (1 Samuel 16:13). And David loved God and trusted Him. During David's reign, Israel prospered. People flourished. They were no longer in Egypt. By God's mighty hand, they left behind bricks and slave masters. Jesse's son, and the nation God built through him, had the appearance of a sturdy tree, not a stump.

Then Israel forgot God; they began to live as if the deliverance had never happened, as if all their gains were self-gotten. Their faith and worship were heartless. They loved idols. God asked, "Is there a God besides Me?" (Isaiah 44:8). With love He warned, "All who fashion idols are nothing, and the things they delight in do not profit" (v. 9). Do parents enjoy punishing their children? No, but loving parents will do so to humble the hearts of their children, to return them to the better path, to awaken them to see clearly God's gifts, His cross, and their place in His family. The Israelites were in a trancelike state, and God would not lose them even if it meant having to swing Babylon like an ax to cut them down, to turn His nation into a stump, the stump of Jesse.

It is amazing how quickly we, too, forget. Forgetting God's goodness is in keeping with *Satan's tyranny*, a sign that we are descendants of sinful Adam. I pray I will not forget a Sunday meal our friends in Romania served to the four of us who had come to visit the pastor, his family, and the congregation we were so fortunate to have been asked to help. That meal included fresh pork cutlets. It had not occurred to me the day before, when walking past a man who was butchering a pig, that it was for the next day's feast—fresh vegetables, homemade bread, and fresh pork—flavorful and unforgettable. The meal was delicious. Fourteen years have passed since that hot, six-day stay. There was no air conditioning, and half the houses didn't have electricity. We washed with water in a porcelain bowl outside the front stoop, near the outhouse. I digress. I remember that meal, especially the words—because there were none. We were enjoying the food amid stories, laughs, and the translation of Romanian to English and vice versa. But when I quietly asked the devoted pastor of the small village, "How often do your people enjoy a meal like this, with such delicious meat?" he did not respond. He heard me, but he would not look at me. He gave no answer, no words. I felt stupid. Many of the families in the little town had a couple of cows or a pig or a number of geese for the down feathers. How many animals did the family have who gave this one to feed us?

Not only do I easily forget God's goodness, but also I am slow to learn that every idol I love is a liar (Isaiah 44:20). Every idol lures me away from God. How can I be so foolish as to crave momentary happiness more than everlasting salvation? Here is a good prayer for me and perhaps for you: "Lord, if need be, turn me into a stump. Have enough mercy to knock me down in order to raise me up with faith in You." Hannah's prayer assures us that God will do this (1 Samuel 2:6–8).

Out of a stump of a nation that was good as dead, that had forgotten all the good that God does, God's mercy would fill the earth. He would bring forth a shoot, a branch, a human being unlike any before or after, who would come from Jesse, from

David, and who would be greater than Solomon (Matthew 12:42). He would come to deliver His people from *Satan's tyranny*. He would come *to save* and to *give them vict'ry o'er the grave*. Indeed, we have reason to sing! *Rejoice! Rejoice! Emmanuel shall come to thee, O Israel!*

5
O come, Thou Key of David, come,
And open wide our heav'nly home;
Make safe the way that leads on high,
And close the path to misery.
Refrain
Rejoice! Rejoice! Emmanuel
Shall come to thee, O Israel!

O Come, Thou Key of David, Come

Maybe you should not name your son *Shebna*. The Lord is slow to anger (Exodus 34:6; Numbers 14:18; Psalm 86:15; Joel 2:13), but regarding the king's steward, Isaiah prophesies, "The LORD will hurl you away violently. . . . He will . . . whirl you around and around, and throw you like a ball into a wide land. There you shall die" (Isaiah 22:17–18). Shebna craved notoriety. He was haughty and self-absorbed and was chastised. He commissioned an elaborate tomb for himself, valued glorious chariots, and failed to use the resources placed under his key for the good of the people. God called him "shame of your master's house" (v. 18), brought punishment, and replaced him. He said of Eliakim, the son of Hilkiah, "He shall be a father to the inhabitants of Jerusalem. . . . I will place on his shoulder the key of the house of David. He shall open, and none shall shut; and he shall shut, and none shall open" (vv. 21–22). The Lord selects the lesser-known story of Shebna, Eliakim, and the one-time Old Testament reference to the key of David to point to Himself when He addresses the church in Philadelphia. He instructs John to write, "The words of the holy one, the true one, who has the key of David, who opens and no one will shut, who shuts and no one opens" (Revelation 3:7). God entrusted Eliakim with complete authority. No one could override his decisions. He held the key of control to open and shut the doors of the king's resources for the good of the king and his people. The Lord Jesus becomes a greater Eliakim, the ultimate steward with the key of control over our eternal well-being. He holds the key to open and shut the door into heaven and the door into hell for you and for me, for everyone.

The matter makes me think of another event. God had told His servant Noah to construct a 450-foot vessel with one door (Genesis 6:16) and no side doors (John 10:9; 14:6; Acts 4:12). After Noah and the animals entered the ark, the Lord sealed the door shut (Genesis 7:16). God was clear. "I will bring a flood of waters upon the earth to destroy all flesh in which is the breath of life under heaven. Everything that is on the earth shall die" (6:17). Noah could not have been the only one to have heard the warning. Genesis does not record conversations between Noah and passersby, but given Noah's faith and the monumental scope of the project, surely people inquired, and he testified. God shut Noah, his wife, and their three sons and their wives safely inside the ark. Inside, is life. Outside, there is no life. No one could reach in to take them out. No one could open the door God had shut to let themselves in. "In the six hundredth year of Noah's life, in the second month, on the seventeenth day of the month, on that day all the fountains of the great deep burst forth, and the windows of the heavens were opened" (Genesis 7:11).

And now the Lord has placed upon His Church (Matthew 16:19; 18:18; John 20:22–23), upon His people and pastors, the responsibility, *the key of David*, the power of His Word to *open wide our heav'nly home* for others, to *make safe* for others *the way that leads on high*. Pastors preach and witness and teach. God places His words on their lips—I forgive you all your sins—to open wide His door to heaven. God equips all of His children. With God's Word, you can respond to someone who cannot believe that God would forgive even him (Psalm 130:3–4), or that He cares about her (Luke 12:7). With the words of Scripture, you can reassure the one who has a flimsy excuse for not approaching the Lord's Table to receive His Holy Meal for the forgiveness of sins (Ecclesiastes 7:20; Jeremiah 17:23; John 3:19). Your pastor is eager to assist you in forming a good reply with God's Word for any person of concern.

The Key of David, the Lord Jesus Himself, has closed the path to our eternal misery and opened wide *our heav'nly home.* Shockingly, mercifully, He did not use a key. He used a cross. *Rejoice! Rejoice! Emmanuel shall come to thee, O Israel!*

> 6 O come, Thou Dayspring from on high,
> And cheer us by Thy drawing nigh;
> Disperse the gloomy clouds of night,
> And death's dark shadows put to flight.
> *Refrain*
> Rejoice! Rejoice! Emmanuel
> Shall come to thee, O Israel!

O Come, Thou Dayspring from On High

The couple prayed for a new day, a dayspring. Zechariah and Elizabeth were descendants of Israel's first high priest, Aaron, who 1,500 years earlier had spoken for Moses before Pharaoh. Their lives were anchored in faith. They lived humbly before God and took His commandments to heart. Even so, whatever privilege might have come with an Aaronic lineage could not fill a gaping void. Elizabeth was barren. They had no children. It was her cross, their cross, to bear. Unlike us, who rely upon retirement plans and care facilities, people back then relied upon children to provide for them when they could no longer provide for themselves. Unless they couldn't. Zechariah and Elizabeth were denied the joy of being parents. In addition, who would care for them? The day they had prayed for had not come, but old age had (Luke 1:5–7). Then the day that could not come *did*.

Zechariah's privilege as a priest was to supply fresh incense to the altar in front of the Most Holy Place. It was in that place that Zechariah had an extraordinary experience. When God uses His angels as messengers—"messenger" is a definition of *angel*—He sometimes sends them in visible bodily form. An angel appeared to Zechariah. He was startled and afraid, understandably. The angel said, "Do not be afraid, Zechariah, for your prayer has been heard, and your wife Elizabeth will bear you a son, and you shall call his name John" (Luke 1:11–13). Zechariah doubted the angel's good news because of their old age, but he learned that God's Word accomplishes what it says. For his doubt, he was made unable to speak, temporarily, a condition serving also as a gracious sign that the announcement was from the Lord (vv. 18–20).

The new day God gave to Zechariah and Elizabeth would bring much more than earthly joy to the aged parents, now no longer barren. Their dayspring is directly related to the new day that gave all of mankind a reason to rejoice. In time, Zechariah and Elizabeth's son, John, prepared to meet not another "prophet of the Most High" but the very "Son of the Most High" (Luke 1:14–17, 32). John knew, "He who is mightier than I is coming" (Luke 3:16), and he would "go before the Lord . . . to give knowledge of salvation to His people in the forgiveness of their sins" (1:76–77). Forgiveness is not received where God has not worked repentance, and John preached it (Luke 3:3). He kept on confronting Herod for his adultery (Matthew 14:4), and he called out the crowds who believed in theory but not in practice, "You brood of vipers! . . . Bear fruit in keeping with repentance" (3:7–8). For his faithfulness, he was met with a grizzly execution (14:10), a further indication of the path the Lord Himself would follow.

Zechariah is blessed to know that his son would "give knowledge of salvation . . . in the forgiveness of their sins, because of the tender mercy of our God, whereby the sunrise shall visit us from on high" (Luke 1:77–78). And there, finally, is this stanza's theme—sunrise. Translated in our hymn, the word is *Dayspring,* a new day, the sunrise that comes from above "to give light to those who sit in darkness and in the shadow of death, to guide our feet into the way of peace" (1:79). When Jesus comes, He brings a day unlike all others. Scripture supports this:

- It is a new day when the angel said to the shepherds at night, "Fear not. . . . For unto you is born *this day* . . . a Savior, who is Christ the Lord." (Luke 2:10–11)

- It is a new day when Jesus said to the sinful woman, "Your sins are forgiven" and to the cheating tax collector, "*Today* salvation has come to this house." (Luke 7:48; 19:9, emphasis added)

- It is a new day when Jesus promises one criminal, "*Today* you will be with Me in paradise." (Luke 23:43, emphasis added)

- It is a new day on "the *first day* of the week, at *early dawn*" when the women found the tomb empty of Jesus' body. (Luke 24:1–3, emphasis added)

- It is a new day after a long night of bad fishing when, "just *as day* was breaking," Jesus served His disciples grilled fish for breakfast, the third time they see Him after He was raised from the dead. (John 21:3–14, emphasis added)

During Advent, let us thank God for bringing to us a new day, even the Dayspring of salvation. And let us ask Him to make us like John the Baptist to bring to others a new day of joy and forgiveness in the name of the One who is drawing nigh! *Rejoice! Rejoice! Emmanuel shall come to thee, O Israel!*

7 O come, Desire of nations, bind
In one the hearts of all mankind;
Bid Thou our sad divisions cease,
And be Thyself our King of Peace.
Refrain
Rejoice! Rejoice! Emmanuel
Shall come to thee, O Israel!

O Come, Desire
of Nations, Bind

This stanza is built upon God's fierce warning and double promise through His prophet Haggai:

> And I will shake all nations, and the desire of all nations shall come: and I will fill this house with glory, saith the LORD of hosts. (Haggai 2:7 KJV)

The Lord of hosts is a name that expresses God's universal authority and power. Haggai cites it fourteen times in two chapters. *The Lord of hosts* is the mighty warrior who defends His people. *Hosts* is the translation of the Hebrew word *Sabaoth*, which we sing in the Sanctus in the Service of the Sacrament and in hymns such as *A Mighty Fortress Is Our God*:

> Ask ye, Who is this?
> Jesus Christ it is,
> Of Sabaoth Lord,
> And there's none other God;
> He holds the field forever. (*LSB* 656:2)

Sabaoth means "hosts" or "armies" and refers to both earthly armies (1 Samuel 17:45; Isaiah 13:4) and heavenly angels (1 Kings 22:19; 2 Kings 6:17). The Lord of *Sabaoth/hosts/armies* holds the spiritual and physical battlefields forever. Haggai knows that the Lord's kill radius, to use military speak, is unlimited. God's Old Testament children need not have feared the Persian Empire, and we know that when the Lord returns to shake the earth (Haggai 2:6, 20–22; Matthew 24:29–31), there will remain only one kingdom whose King is the protecting, universal governance, the Lord of hosts. Self-directed delusional rulers and nations act as if the Lord does not exist, but they have set themselves up like "scarecrows in a cucumber field" (Jeremiah 10:5). Their denial of the Lord of hosts will cease.

> But the LORD is the true God; He is the living God and the everlasting King. At His wrath the earth quakes, and the nations cannot endure His indignation. (Jeremiah 10:10)

Not only does Haggai warn the nations who plot in vain, but he also warns people who had ambition to build luxurious houses. Shouldn't they have desired to restore the Lord's holy temple too (Haggai 1:2, 4)? Haggai likens an unfaithful laborer to one who puts his wages into a bag with holes (v. 6). This is the kind of emptiness that fills the hearts of all who fail to fear, love, and trust in God above all things. Advent, with royal blue or purple paraments, signals our sure hope for the King of peace to come and our reason for repentance; it is the Lord of hosts we are about to meet. We might want to check our own pockets for holes.

When the Lord of hosts, the *Desire of nations*, comes He brings peace, *shalom*, except for unbelievers—there will be no peace for them (Isaiah 48:22). For you there is peace because the chastisement ("punishment" in the NIV) that brought it was upon Him (Isaiah 53:5). By His grace, from this earth you will depart in peace, like Simeon (Luke 2:29). Now you have peace with God through Jesus (Romans 5:1) that far exceeds eating and drinking (14:17). Paul prays, asking "the God of hope [to] fill you with all joy and peace in believing" (15:13) that "the root of Jesse will come, even He who arises to rule the Gentiles" (15:12), and knowing that "the God of peace will soon crush Satan under your feet" (16:20). When the *Desire of nations* comes, He will wipe evil off the face of earth, return peace to creation, and restore for His children the harmony of unmarred paradise. When the *Desire of nations* comes, "the wolf shall dwell with the lamb, and the leopard shall lie down with the young goat, and the calf and the lion and the fattened calf together; and a little child shall lead them" (Isaiah 11:6). The Lord will not take back His oath; He will bring peace (Ezekiel 34:25–31). Even now, each Lord's Day, He opens your pastor's mouth to speak Aaron's benediction to give you His peace (Numbers 6:24–26), and Paul writes:

> Now may the Lord of peace Himself give you peace at all times in every way. (2 Thessalonians 3:16)

You may not feel the peace of God in your heart even after reading a broad list of biblical references to the peace that God gives. His peace is surely yours. God nailed His own Son mercilessly in order to secure your peace with Him eternally. He truly is your *King of Peace! Rejoice! Rejoice! Emmanuel shall come to thee, O Israel!*

Where Shepherds Lately Knelt

1 Where shepherds lately knelt and kept the
    angel's word,
I come in half-belief, a pilgrim strangely
    stirred;
But there is room and welcome there for me,
But there is room and welcome there for me.

2 In that unlikely place I find Him as they said:
Sweet newborn babe, how frail! And in a
    manger bed:
A still, small voice to cry one day for me,
A still, small voice to cry one day for me.

3 How should I not have known Isaiah would
    be there,
  His prophecies fulfilled? With pounding heart
    I stare:
  A child, a son, the Prince of Peace for me,
  A child, a son, the Prince of Peace for me.

4 Can I, will I forget how Love was born,
    and burned
  Its way into my heart—unasked, unforced,
    unearned,
  To die, to live, and not alone for me,
  To die, to live, and not alone for me?

LSB 369
TEXT: JAROSLAV J. VAJDA (1919–2008); COPYRIGHT © 1986 CPH

"here Shepherds Lately Knelt" is a remarkable gift, but it is easily missed because it is placed a third of the way into our hymnal's Christmas section. Across the page are the soaring notes for the "Glo-ri-a" from "Angels We Have Heard on High." Before and after it are favorites such as "Away in a Manger," "Silent Night," "Joy to the World," and "O Come, All Ye Faithful." Is it necessary to squeeze in another Christmas hymn? Maybe not "necessary," but it is helpful. This hymn takes our doubts, weaknesses, and pains directly to the world's key event, where we ponder its impact upon our lives and other people's. Most of all, this remarkable hymn brings Christmas peace.

The following devotions expound upon distinguishing marks within each stanza. Before we go there, though, we pause here to recognize the significance of the relationship between a given hymn's text and its tune—a key component of this hymn in particular—as well as several creative musical and literary nuances that help make it a welcome gift.

We know right away whether we like a hymn's melody. We know whether we find comfort and strength in the hymn's words. However, we may not often think about how helpful it is when a hymn's tune and text complement each other, when the melody embraces the words and message as if they were one. When thinking of "Holy, Holy, Holy," for example, we may say the words to ourselves while humming or whistling the melody. It is not by chance when a melody augments the message and assists carrying it into our minds and hearts. By way of contrast, imagine singing phrases such as "all is calm" and "holy infant so tender and mild" to the melody of "Thy Strong Word," with the confident downbeats and the thirteen staccato-like triplets (the singing of three quarter notes in the space of time meant for two), instead of the gently flowing musical lines of "Silent Night." Or imagine it the other way around, singing these three words, "Thy strong Word," with the beginning notes of "Silent Night." Sense the awkwardness of hearing those notes and words together. It does not work, not merely because it is not the tune we are accustomed to singing with these words, but also because the *meaning* of the phrase "Thy strong Word" does not match the *style* of the tune STILLE NACHT. For many hymns, the words and melody were written independently of each other. After an author has penned the words, an existing tune that matches well is assigned to it. There are other instances when the author has the melody before writing the text or when the composer has the text before writing the tune. "Where Shepherds Lately Knelt" is a fine example of the latter. After studying the author's message, the composer began his craft of enhancing the hymn's meaning through the notes, musical phrases, and melody he wrote. He even took liberty to alter the author's meter, the number of syllables per line. Originally, the hymn's meter was 6.6.6.6.4.4.2. But the composer recognized the importance of the final three short phrases and the repetition of "for me" at each stanza's end, so he divided seven lines into three and repeated the last line, resulting in 12.12.10.10 (Vajda, 166).

Using *for me* to complete each stanza is a prominent feature of this hymn. To help this ending make a greater impact, the author chose to relay the Bethlehem event from his own vantage point by using the first-person pronoun *I* six times. This additional literary feature is highly unusual and very effective. There are 34 other Christmas hymns in *Lutheran Service Book*. *I* appears in only 8 of them, in only 14 of 145 stanzas, for a total of 20 times. This includes the three times the angel in "From Heaven Above to Earth I Come" announces his Good News to every home.

We expect *I* in hymns of repentance. "Lord, to You I make confession: I have sinned and gone astray, I have multiplied transgression, Chosen for myself my way" (*LSB* 608). Or the sobering lines of Luther's justification hymn may come to mind: "Fast bound in Satan's chains I lay; Death brooded darkly o'er me. Sin was my torment night and day; In sin my mother bore me. But daily deeper still I fell; My life became a living hell, So firmly sin possessed me" (*LSB* 556:2).

Christmas hymns announce Jesus' birth and proclaim what He has come to do. There was no *I* in the angel's Christmas Eve message: "For unto you is born this day in the city of David a Savior, who is Christ the Lord" (Luke 2:11) or in Luke's report: "And suddenly there was with the angel a multitude of the heavenly host praising God and saying, 'Glory to God in the highest'" (2:13).

So why use first person for this hymn? The author wanted to prevent our Christmas pilgrimage from becoming routine or sentimental (Vajda, 165–66). Writing from his viewpoint would provide a fresh approach but also create a serious challenge: *How do we sing about ourselves six times in four stanzas without covering up Christ?*

In "Dear Christians One and All Rejoice" (*LSB* 556) quoted above, Luther models Christ-centered first-person writing by describing himself (and us) by our inherited fallen nature. His cries of desperation—"Fast bound in Satan's chains I lay" and "daily deeper still I fell"—reveal our helplessness without Christ. The simple language in the children's hymn "God Loves Me Dearly" also articulates our need for the Savior and explains what He came to do. "I was in slavery, Sin, death, and darkness" (*LSB* 392:2) and "Jesus, my Savior, Paid all I owed" (st. 4). The author of "Where Shepherds Lately Knelt" uses *I* statements in a different style but for the same purpose—to show our need for God's Son and to proclaim why He has come. Here is a preview of the relationship between *I* and *for me* in each stanza. After the opening phrase, *Where shepherds lately knelt and kept the angel's word*, the author reveals:

I come in half-belief.

It may be half-belief, literally, that we experience, or perhaps lasting regret or even heavy anxiety accompanies us as we make our way to the manger. Singing with the author makes the refrain profoundly meaningful: *But there is room and welcome there for me.*

Stanza 2, then, implies surprise and delight, *In that unlikely place I find Him as they said*, and announces why He came:

A still, small voice to cry one day for me.

Next, stanza 3 adds a surprise in the form of a question with an amazing revelation:

How should I not have known Isaiah would be there?

The author rejoices in Old Testament prophecies: "Behold, the virgin shall conceive and bear a son" (Isaiah 7:14) and "For to us a child is born, to us a son is given; and the government shall be upon His shoulder, and His name shall be called Wonderful Counselor, Mighty God, Everlasting Father, Prince of Peace" (9:6). And at the other side of that prophecy, after its fulfillment, the hymn's author describes himself, *with pounding heart I stare,* kneeling next to the object of his gaze:

A child, a son, the Prince of Peace for me.

Finally, with two more *I* statements and the concluding *for me* in stanza 4, the author focuses on the path of the shepherds, who "made known the saying that had been told them concerning this child" (Luke 2:17). The shepherds could not keep the Good News to themselves. The Gospel does not lie dormant in the hearts of God's children. The author asks:

Can I, will I forget how Love was born . . .
To die, to live, and not alone for me?

The Tune and Text Work Together

With his tune MANGER SONG, the composer expresses the mood and meaning of the text. The gently flowing first two musical lines do not impede the corresponding opening words of each stanza. An interesting side point worth mentioning here is that to create this less dominant, tender feel in the melody, the first note is the "leading tone," the note a half step below the key note. Hymn tunes often have a strong defined beginning, which typically relates to the key. For example, sung in the key of G, three of the first four notes in "O Come, All Ye Faithful" are G. Using a dominant opening interval as in "Lift High the Cross" or "The Advent of Our God" is another strong way to begin a hymn and to establish the key. In "Where Shepherds Lately Knelt," beginning the half step below the key note and avoiding the primary note at the start of the second line accomplishes two things. It helps create the musical style and feel the composer sought to complement the text, and it marks a contrast with the musical third line to give the refrain more attention.

Granted, attempting to describe what music is trying to say is a highly subjective venture. Even so, the composer's skill in accentuating the third line is difficult to miss or overstate. The third line is vivid, like a bell, and brings home at each stanza's end the beautiful thought *for me*. At the start of the third line, the key note repeats three times ahead of a dramatic interval, which reaches the important fourth word of each stanza, *room*, *voice*, *son*, and *live*. That high note repeats four times and ascends one more step to reach the word *for*. The musical line cannot stop there, and neither can the sentence. Musically, that note feels like taking in a breath and waiting to breathe out. The note needs to resolve. It needs to land. It cannot hang suspended. And so it is with the preposition. *For* requires an answer. *There is room and welcome there* . . . for whom? Six times we sing of ourselves, each time preparing us for the truth. The truth is what the shepherds heard the angels say and what the shepherds saw where they knelt. It is what the still, small voice would cry, and precisely what Isaiah foretold seven centuries earlier. The truth is that Christmas is not about me. The truth is that Christmas brings peace because Christ is for me.

> 1 Where shepherds lately knelt and kept the
>   angel's word,
>   I come in half-belief, a pilgrim strangely
>   stirred;
>   But there is room and welcome there for me,
>   But there is room and welcome there for me.

I Come in Half-Belief,
a Pilgrim Strangely Stirred

We do not sing what we might expect to sing in response to the opening of the hymn, *Where shepherds lately knelt and kept the angel's word*. We do not sing something like *I come in full delight, the Good News having heard*. No, we sing *I come in half-belief*. Half-belief? Imagine singing, instead of *O come, all ye faithful*, this: *O come, half-believers*. Or instead of *Joy to the world, the Lord is come!* rather, *Joy to the world, with half-belief* . . . Who sings with half-belief at Christmas? Perhaps those who have not been permitted to admit it? Maybe I'm wrongly interpreting the author's heart and intent. Maybe he does not mean half-belief literally, but awe and wonder. But if so, then the repeated last phrase should be something like *I long to see my Savior there for me*. As is, the conjunction *but* and the last phrase clarify the author's position. *But there is room and welcome there for me* means, despite the author's uncertainty, the Savior welcomes him.

Maybe half-belief is not an issue for you. If your faith and trust let you kneel by the manger without doubt, then you are blessed. But there are others who well know half-belief or even a total flooding of uncertainty yet are thankful to kneel and to know *there is room and welcome* from the Savior who will not send them away. For some, *half-belief* pertains to doubt driven by questions of science: Adam was formed from dirt? A global flood?

Christ rose and will visibly, physically return? He will raise all the dead? Some who doubt mean no mockery. They pray for strong faith. They have memorized Mark 9:24 and will sing this hymn in full voice. *But there is room and welcome there for me.*

For others, doubt is driven by unpleasant circumstance and pain. Some are ready to say, "My life is a mess. God is with me? I can hardly believe it." Some people long for His closeness, for His comfort, but can't help wonder if He has left them. They feel unworthy for doubting. Perhaps your half-belief is not related to doubting miracles or to the presence of pain. Perhaps it is tied to your sin. You have heard the pastor say, dozens of times, hundreds of times: "I forgive you all your sins, in the name of the Father . . . ," and you can't completely believe it. Guilt does not go away. There were those late nights in your early twenties or the hours you cheated the time clock. Perhaps you are getting up in years, and all the living you did doesn't mean much now. You regret having lived so many hours and days for only one person, the one standing in your shoes. The problem isn't that you half-believe in God's birth and doubt His return; the problem is that you fear it. You fear His judgment. You only half-believe that you won't get the eternal damnation you deserve. You half-believe you will get it! You have difficulty imagining that you will end up in the same good place as other people you have known to be so giving, so sacrificing. In short, it is difficult for you to believe that God really did send His Son to take the eternal punishment you deserve and to give you eternal peace with Him.

Sing, and take to heart the words of the beautiful refrain. *But there is room and welcome there for me.*

Can we be sure? Yes, we can. Think about what happened. An angel of the Lord spoke to the shepherds, "Fear not. . . . For unto you is born this day in the city of David a Savior, who is Christ the Lord" (Luke 2:10–11). Two words make a remarkable difference. *Born* and *Savior*—those two words are important, true, but they are not the words I mean. Without the other two words, there is no certainty. The Christmas message is not vague. Christmas peace is not implied; it is certain. "Fear not. . . . For *unto you* is born this day in the city of David a Savior." The shepherds

understood the packed sentence. It is personal. *Unto you* leaves
no doubt. *Unto you* means this:

> But there is room and welcome there for me,
> But there is room and welcome there for me.

> 2 In that unlikely place I find Him
> as they said:
> Sweet newborn babe, how frail! And in
> a manger bed:
> A still, small voice to cry one day for me,
> A still, small voice to cry one day for me.

In That Unlikely Place
I Find Him as They Said

The author draws us to the days of King Herod and to the scene of the manger bed. We praise God for the angel's message, "This will be a sign for you: you will find a baby wrapped in swaddling cloths and lying in a manger" (Luke 2:12). That message, that Word from God, makes it possible to discern the significance of the setting. The setting is God's sign. The manger and cloths are like God's banner telling all that *this* is the Child who is come to save us. The *still, small voice* of *this* baby will *cry one day for me.*

We are familiar with Jesus' cries from the cross. At about three o'clock in the afternoon, Jesus cried out with a loud voice, "Eli, Eli" (Matthew 27:46). Those are human words cried by a human Son to His Father. You've made that cry too. Perhaps with an emphatic "O" preceding "my God!" you cried for help. The doctor's gentle voice bears the worst news, and "O my God" comes out of your heart, a moment of true prayer, not the cheap, flipping of God's name in vain as is popular—no, not when the knees have buckled, not when the words "my God" are followed by an exclamatory "No!" or "Why?" No matter the circumstance, when you cry to God, He is already working His will for your good, for the good of others, for the strengthening of your faith and the keeping of your soul. For you, God is near, not far off (Isaiah 43:2), and He has paradise waiting for you or for a brother or sister in Christ when He allows a breath to be the last (Luke 23:43).

Jesus, however, who trusted and honored His Father, is abandoned, forsaken, eternally forgotten by Him. Jesus is damned. "Eli, Eli, lema sabachthani" identifies incomprehensible suffering of a man, a human. Our Brother cried "My God!" when squeezed by shame, pain, and dehumanizing forsakenness. His divinity did not protect Him from human agony. He pleaded to His Father. His Father did not ignore Him. His Father left Him, abandoned Him. He crushed Him (Isaiah 53:10).

The cry of forsakenness reveals that Jesus is a man and what He suffered as a man. There is another cry He makes from the cross, His last one, which reveals His majesty and His divinity. "Jesus cried out again with a loud voice and yielded up His spirit" (Matthew 27:50). The *still, small voice* is not so small after all. When a loved one dies, the breathing often slows and shallows. Speech stops. Bodily movements diminish to light twitches. The eyes no longer open. There is decline until there is nothing. At that moment, in such a state, can you imagine Grandma crying out in a loud voice? A crucified man struggles for hours for every single breath. The lungs and body collapse. Sometimes, the guards break legs to prevent a pushing up to open up the chest cavity for airflow. A crucified man does not die with an outcry. Rather, he cannot cry or breathe or yell at all.

Again, consider this: "He cried out with a loud voice and yielded up His spirit" (Matthew 27:50). Death is not in command. Jesus is. "No one takes it from Me, but I lay it down of My own accord. . . . I have authority to take it up again" (John 10:18). It was that way all along. The Creator is in control. He calms the seas (Matthew 8:26) and tells demons where to go (8:32). He multiplies fish for the multitudes (Mark 6:41–42), walks on water (6:48), and healed the one who touched His garment (6:56). When the time was right, He "set His face to go to Jerusalem" (Luke 9:51). He determined the time for the disciples to depart from the meal they shared together and to sing a hymn (Mark 14:26). He insisted that Peter put away the sword, and He refused to counter the scorn at the cross, "You who would destroy the temple and rebuild it in three days, save Yourself. If You are the Son of God, come down" (Matthew 27:40). Instead, He submitted. He cried out in a loud voice, and He yielded up His spirit.

When Jesus cried, "My God, My God," He was suffering everything, and He was controlling everything when He cried out and gave up His spirit. He hears and understands your cries. Even more, He controls all outcomes for you.

How should I not have known Isaiah would
   be there,
His prophecies fulfilled? With pounding heart
   I stare:
A child, a son, the Prince of Peace for me,
A child, a son, the Prince of Peace for me.

How Should I Not Have Known Isaiah Would Be There

Isaiah reaches Bethlehem with faith's eye and prophecy seven hundred years in advance. We kneel with the author to envision not only the sign from God, the baby in the manger, but also Isaiah and all the departed saints, prophets, apostles, and martyrs who gather with the angels to praise God for the birth of the Prince of Peace. Our short-term separation from those who are now with the Lord in glory does not diminish the greater reality: All who are in Christ, on earth and in heaven, are joined together in the unending praise of God (Revelation 7:9–17).

The author names Isaiah because his prophecy is cited dozens of times in the New Testament, more than any other prophet, by Matthew, Mark, Luke, John, and Paul. We are amazed by Isaiah's Christmas prophecy pointing to Jesus, born of a virgin. He is Immanuel (Isaiah 7:14; Matthew 1:23), the Son given unto us, "Wonderful Counselor, Mighty God, Everlasting Father, Prince of Peace" (Isaiah 9:6). Every Good Friday, Christians worldwide hear in precise detail the prophet's foretelling of our Lord's Passion:

> He was crushed for our iniquities; upon Him
> was the chastisement that brought us peace.
> (Isaiah 53:5)

Isaiah also uses blistering reprimands to humble us, to accuse and convict, to cause us to remain repentant and dependent upon the Lord. He counters them with some of the most comforting and certain promises of grace, forgiveness, and everlasting life spoken in all of Scripture.

Here is a sample of his convict-comfort and accuse-forgive proclamation. In Isaiah 1:10–17, the prophet equates God's people in faithlessness to the "rulers of Sodom" and the "people of Gomorrah." He rejects their worship and offerings as heartless, as a thankless going through the motions. He warns that when they fold their hands in prayer, God will not listen. Is Isaiah speaking to us too? Take a moment to consider where God is in your own heart and in the lives of your children and friends. For many, the 2008 Great Recession seems long gone and not that great. When comfortable income meets decent health, it may be difficult to remain grateful to God, focused upon helping others, and intent upon bringing Christ to those without Him. But the One who gives the gifts does not want them to become a source of spiritual stupor. Those who recklessly feed a passion for entertainment and pleasure risk that God will no longer listen when they pray, meaning, how can sincere prayers come from a person with dead faith? What is there for God to hear? Isaiah's warning should startle us.

In keeping with his structure, Isaiah then announces grace and mercy unexpectedly, immediately, and clearly:

> Come now, let us reason together, says the LORD:
> though your sins are like scarlet, they shall be as
> white as snow; though they are red like crimson,
> they shall become like wool. (Isaiah 1:18)

We have glanced at Isaiah's first chapter. There are sixty-five more. You could spend additional time with him during the next year. Consider working with these key chapters: 6; 25; 35; 40; 43; 53; 55; 60; 65. Perhaps you own a study Bible—look to helpful footnotes. They are brief and easily understood. And ask questions of your pastor.

With pounding heart I stare.

How could the author's heart not pound? He knows the baby's hands and feet will be mangled with nails for his sins to secure his salvation. This Christmas, gaze upon the manger; sense the shepherds' awe at the fulfillment of the angel's word. Even more, take to heart and pass to others the gifts the Savior has wrapped for you in the voice of His prophet Isaiah. With these words, God has been sustaining the faith of His people for 2,700 years:

> Behold, God is my salvation; I will trust, and will
> not be afraid; for the LORD GOD is my strength
> and my song, and He has become my salvation.
> (Isaiah 12:2)

> The grass withers, the flower fades, but the word of
> our God will stand forever. (Isaiah 40:8)

> He will tend His flock like a shepherd; He will
> gather the lambs in His arms; He will carry them
> in His bosom, and gently lead those that are with
> young. (Isaiah 40:11)

The promises continue! You will be encouraged by reading the following:

- Isaiah 43:1–2

- Isaiah 44:6

- Isaiah 49:15

- Isaiah 55:10–11

> 4 Can I, will I forget how Love was born,
>   and burned
>   Its way into my heart—unasked,
>   unforced, unearned,
>   To die, to live, and not alone for me,
>   To die, to live, and not alone for me?

How Love Was Born,
and Burned

—————

Thirty some years ago when Dr. Dale Meyer was our seminary homiletics professor, he said, "Write a sermon about evangelism without using the word *evangelism*." Befuddled, we sort of responded with a collective "Huh?" He did not add, "Instead of the word *evangelism*, use a synonymous word or phrase such as 'witness' or 'spread the Good News' or 'tell others what Jesus has done for you.'" No, he said something like, "Make the Gospel sound so good that your people can't wait to tell someone. That's the best kind of evangelism sermon."

The fourth stanza of our hymn makes the Gospel sound good by using five words: *born, burned, unasked, unforced, unearned*.

A congregation in Houston was having a missions festival. I attended as part of a seminary quartet. We sang in the program that was held outside in the courtyard. Children were seated on the ground. As I recall, a wealthy man sat with them, chatting, smiling, cracking open peanuts. He appeared to be in his seventies, and the children were elementary students. How many rich men in suit pants sit on the bare ground, cracking peanuts with young children? I think he learned their names too. The children did not ask him to join them, such a distinguished, intimidating looking fellow, and he did not force his way into their hearts.

But they sure took to him; they saw his care for them and his love for missions.

Can I forget how Love was born, and burned Its way into my heart? The rich man, the only Son of God, sat down in Bethlehem; He was *born* in the likeness of men, emptying Himself (Philippians 2:7). He even became sin for us (2 Corinthians 5:21). In Jerusalem, everyone saw the rich man's love for missions. He carried His own cross before they nailed Him to it. There He completed His mission to take our sin in order to give us paradise. On that first Easter afternoon, the two disciples' hearts *burned* within them as a stranger explained how the Old Testament pointed to the Savior (Luke 24:13–27).

Which Bible stories are most helpful to you—Abraham offering Isaac, Elijah and the Baal prophets, Christmas, Jesus calming the storm, Jesus raising Lazarus, the Lord's Passion, His resurrection, perhaps the work of Peter and Paul in Acts? They all pertain to our meditation here, and this is certain: God promises to ignite faith and to keep it burning brightly through the hearing of Scripture.

Unasked? At the moment physical life begins, there is no spiritual life, no fear, love, and trust in God, no living relationship with the Creator, no faith. God is the giver of life. Physical life is received *unasked.* Likewise, spiritual life, faith in God, together with all of His grace, is received *unasked.* What about when someone becomes a Christian as an adult and thinks, "I accepted Jesus as my Savior"? Experientially, or psychologically, this is how it seems, but actually, the conversion of an adult marks the work God has accomplished through His living Word spoken by a friend, spouse, relative, or colleague, heard in worship or read on a Christmas card (Romans 10:14–17). This is what Luther meant in his explanation of the Third Article of the Apostles' Creed: "I cannot by my own reason or strength believe in Jesus Christ, my Lord, or come to Him, but the Holy Spirit has called me by the Gospel." Luther understood Paul, who taught, "No one can say 'Jesus is Lord' except in the Holy Spirit" (1 Corinthians 12:3). Here is the beautiful thing about the truth of how conversion takes place: There is so much comfort in knowing that God created faith and sustains it in me rather than in needing to rely on the strength of my convictions and decisions!

Unforced? God does not force His love upon us. He keeps giving and showing it. The grace you received in Baptism will never dry up; He welcomes you to His Holy Supper, always, and He continually gives you access to His Holy Word!

Unearned? Does this need a comment? When a friend insinuates, "I have earned His favor," a good reply with a little smile is, "On what planet are you living?" Then follow with, "I mean, really, how, exactly, have you done that?"

The first stanza's Christmas promise is so good! Even with doubts and half-belief, there is *welcome there for me!* And just in case one forgets that the news is too good to keep, the fourth stanza asks a question. The question does not guilt or corner me. It does not use the word *evangelism.* It coaxes me to tell others. It gently inspires me to want to share the Christmas promises. Can I forget that Jesus was born *to die, to live, and not alone for me?*

Give Ear, O Zion, to God's Call

1 Give ear, O Zion, to God's call,
And hearken, chosen nation:
God comes with righteousness for all,
With mercy and salvation;
God comes with comfort for your gloom,
Until your desert places bloom
With thankful songs of gladness.

2 Behold, God bares His holy arm,
His Servant to us sending;
God clothed in flesh need not alarm,
He comes our race befriending:
A Lamb in whom no sin is found,
Yet bearing ours, He makes no sound
As He is led to slaughter.

3 Our death upon the cross He died,
Yet see—this Lamb is living!
In Christ, we now stand justified,
His guiltlessness us giving!
Out of the anguish of His soul,
We have been cleansed, restored, made whole;
Baptized in Christ, made righteous!

4 Each one of us is robed in white,
Christ's holiness now wearing;
Called out of darkness into light,
God's love in Christ declaring;
We live and die in Jesus' name;
His grace, from yesterday the same,
Today, tomorrow—ever!

5 Look to the heav'ns, lift up your eyes
And understand this clearly:
That this fair earth beneath those skies
And all we love so dearly,
Will one day face its fiery fate;
Like smoke the heav'ns will dissipate
At Jesus' reappearing!

6 What kind of people ought you be
As this Last Day approaches?
In love, rebuke all blasphemy;
Fear not the world's reproaches;
Live godly lives of faithfulness;
Christ's saving work to all confess;
Thus hasten His returning.

7 Sing God the Father's majesty:
Of naught He made creation!
To God the Son all glory be:
His blood wrought our salvation!
The Holy Spirit magnify:
He dwells within to sanctify—
One God Most High forever!

TEXT: STEPHEN P. STARKE, B. 1955

hy an Old Testament sounding title for a twenty-first-century hymn? *Give ear? O Zion?* We do not usually talk like this. Before addressing the spirit of the title, touching on the components of this hymn, and introducing a person God used to deeply influence my faith, here is the story of origin for this hymn.

Thirteen pastors and a century and a half after Rev. Peter Heinrich Dicke met with five German families to form a congregation in the dense forests of northern Wisconsin, our congregation asked hymnwriter Pastor Stephen Starke if he might consider writing a hymn for our 150th anniversary. He graciously accepted and explained that his purpose would not be to write solely for the people of St. Paul, Bonduel, with our local heritage in mind, but to write a hymn centered in Christ, in His grace, and in His saving work for us all. Lord willing, he said, the hymn will be a blessing for the Church, for the people of many congregations, although it was written for a specific occasion.

Our hymn committee selected the tune NUN FREUT EUCH, strong in association with Luther and the Reformation and familiar to many via "Dear Christians, One and All, Rejoice" (*LSB* 556). Regarding a theme and content for the hymn, the committee knew that the hymn must proclaim a bold, sure message of salvation in Christ crucified. And it was mentioned that since our congregation's cemetery holds not only grandpas and grandmas but many children, the hymn could also speak a message of hope and comfort. Finally, the hymn was to include as well the challenge of living as God's children in a culture that has to an alarming extent abandoned God and His Word. In short, these themes—salvation, comfort, and Christian life—and a scriptural starting point (Isaiah 51:1–7) were relayed to Pastor Starke. The hymn we are examining here is the result.

Turning to the hymn, the opening phrase, *Give ear, O Zion, to God's call,* and particularly one word in it, speak the Good News of Christ to all Christians. The word is *Zion*, which means at least three things:

- The people of God

- The place where the Lord dwells

- The place from where the Lord acts for salvation in the future

Bible passages citing this word abound. "Zion hears and is glad" (Psalm 97:8). The inhabitants of Zion shout and sing for joy (Isaiah 12:6). Psalm 48 delivers praise to the Lord because He dwells at Zion. In Lamentations 4:2, the "precious sons of Zion" are "worth their weight in fine gold." An abundance of prophetic promises are ultimately completed for us, the present-day children of Zion, through the work of Jesus Christ:

- Zion shall be redeemed. (Isaiah 1:27)

- He will wash away the filth of our sin. He who is left in Zion will be called holy. (Isaiah 4:3–4)

- In Zion, the Lord will lay a sure foundation, a precious cornerstone, and whoever believes will not flee in terror. (Isaiah 28:16)

- He will secure Zion from its enemies. (Isaiah 33:20)

- The Lord in majesty will be for us a place of life-giving water, and He will save us. (Isaiah 33:21–22)

- He will fill Zion with justice and righteousness. (Isaiah 33:5)

- He will be the abundance of salvation. (Isaiah 33:6)

- Zion will weep no more. (Isaiah 30:19)

- "The LORD comforts Zion," and the land will become as lush and fruitful as the Garden of Eden. "Joy and gladness will be found in her." (Isaiah 51:3)

Give ear, O Zion, to God's call—what a beautiful and powerful opening. The remainder of stanza 1 identifies the Lord's *comfort for your gloom*, His mercy and salvation. All other comfort brings short-lived relief. The next three stanzas also present an array of Christ's works and gifts for us, the people of Zion. God's *holy arm* is a powerful metaphor cited in stanza 2. God is spirit. He has many attributes, but He does not have a body. His *holy arm* is His only Son, and amazingly, *God clothed in flesh need not alarm*. Stanza 3 identifies the Lord's twofold work for us. He surely was crucified in our place; He took the punishment we deserved. He did this only after first living His entire life without sin. His guiltlessness He gives to us now through Baptism. Beautiful baptismal imagery flows throughout stanza 4, excepting the ending, where the author captures our congregation's anniversary theme and suggests the strong relationship between God's glory and God's grace.

Woven throughout the hymn's first twenty-eight lines are the Lord's accomplished and continuous actions to comfort and to save us. At stanza 5, though, the tune for the hymn does not change, but the tone and message change abruptly. It pointedly speaks to Christians living in the world today and reflects the full, twofold message of God. Across Scripture, in the Pentateuch, throughout the Prophets, in the Psalms, in the Gospels, and in the Letters of Paul, there is Gospel—hope, forgiveness, deliverance, salvation, and paradise. But there is also Law—fierce warning of judgment and guidance for life. No one will have trouble discerning the difference in this stanza. The warning is sobering. The Last Day is coming with fire.

Stanza 6 stirs up a sense of urgency for the people of Zion to take action for the sake of our neighbors, who also face the Last Day. In keeping with this hymn's life event—an influential person—I think of and thank God for Viola. Her faith and piety are born not of academic books but of a life with trial, including years under communist rule, and of time with her Lord each day in His Word. She knows that God loves her. It is plain to see how she fears, loves, and trusts Him. She desires to please Him, and I introduce her at stanza 6 because of her unyielding determination to speak to others the saving truth in Christ *as this Last Day approaches.*

The hymn concludes wonderfully with stanza 7, a tightly woven doxological stanza giving acclaim to the Almighty—Father, Son, Holy Spirit—for His unfathomable, creative, saving, and sanctifying work.

Give ear, O Zion, to God's call.

> 1 Give ear, O Zion, to God's call,
> And hearken, chosen nation:
> God comes with righteousness for all,
> With mercy and salvation;
> God comes with comfort for your gloom,
> Until your desert places bloom
> With thankful songs of gladness.

Comfort for Your Gloom

When problems come, we gladly welcome a friend's whisper of heartfelt compassion. It makes us feel loved and not alone. We appreciate the encouragement, even though we are left knowing that empathy does not actually change circumstances. Often, we are incapable of altering and certainly of eliminating the problem. In an admission of weakness, we may invoke the common cliché: "It is what it is." The cliché does not comfort. "It is what it is" means "If I could change it, I would."

When we most need Him, the Creator, who cared so much for us that He came to Bethlehem, comes closer still. As the hymn proclaims, *God comes with righteousness for all, With mercy and salvation.* The promise is sure; it is grounded in His cross, not in a cliché, and it is astonishing. The mercy and salvation He brings reestablishes our point of reference from earth (where we suffer) to heaven (where there is no pain), from the temporal to the eternal.

Yet sometimes the pain we experience overshadows our anticipation of salvation. We have heard or thought, "Yes, the Lord has heaven waiting for me, but I don't know how much more I can take." When our pain lingers or intensifies, the words of God's promises in this stanza become more beautiful because they reassure us of Christ's righteousness and mercy, that He comes with salvation, and that salvation *is* His final solution, His *comfort for your gloom.* Receiving a cure, a cash gift or settlement, or even a string of pleasant days are nice gifts representing an exchange of the desirable for the undesirable, but they will pass. Earthly gifts interrupt pain momentarily. Earthly gifts cannot bring everlasting paradise.

Recall the story of the paralytic from Mark 2:1–12. Quite possibly he understood very well what we sense if our pain seems to outweigh God's promise of salvation. The paralytic's four friends believed Jesus would heal him. But so many people had gathered in the house where Jesus was that there was no room for them to enter. So the friends made an opening in the roof and lowered the man. Jesus saw the faith of the friends and said to the paralyzed man, "Your sins are forgiven" (v. 5). Maybe he was a man of faith, overjoyed at receiving forgiveness. Or perhaps he was thinking, "Sins? *SINS?* What about my legs! I thought I was going to walk, work, and live like a man! I am a fool! A miracle? Not for this paralytic!" Jesus would gladly heal the man, but He was mindful of the dreadful eternal consequences were He not to *forgive* him. Jesus cured his paralysis so he could walk around town; He took away his sins so he would walk in His eternal kingdom.

Jesus brings forgiveness, mercy, and salvation—the real comfort for our gloom. Cling to these gifts! The desert places of pain in our lives are real, and He comes always with comfort, never clichés. He comes with salvation and eternity's peace to swallow our troubles. The One who lived without sin insisted upon taking the punishment for ours, and He promises that the day is coming when our *desert places [will] bloom With thankful songs of gladness.*

2   Behold, God bares His holy arm,
His Servant to us sending;
God clothed in flesh need not alarm,
He comes our race befriending:
A Lamb in whom no sin is found,
Yet bearing ours, He makes no sound
As He is led to slaughter.

God's Arm Revealed

God is not seen. He is spirit, eternal, unchangeable, almighty, all-knowing, present everywhere, holy, just, faithful, good, merciful, and gracious. He is "slow to anger, and abounding in steadfast love" (Exodus 34:6). But He is not seen. We see His work in creation, but we don't see Him. When God spoke, everything that exists began. Martin Luther stressed that God's speaking is the foundation of all reality apart from His person. Ponder that. When God speaks, His words are mighty and lively, dispensing not mere information, but creative power. We see the works—including life-sustaining water, indigo bunting birds, beehives, the Grand Canyon, the morning sun, and above all, human life—but not the Worker. The complexity of deoxyribonucleic acid, or DNA, with its three billion bases attaching to sugar and phosphate molecules making nucleotides arranged in a long ladderlike spiral called a double helix, is a miraculous phenomenon. Life cannot come from nonlife, no matter how many imaginary years the evolutionist offers, and everyone knows it. Living cells are not the fieldstone's offspring. God created matter out of nothing. From the dirt He made, He formed Adam, and into him breathed life.

Evidence of the Creator abounds, but it is only upon revealing His holy arm that the Maker becomes visible. Isaiah's "arm of God" is a metaphor, a figure of speech. God the Father is a personal being, but without a body. He does have a Son. Mary delivered Him in Bethlehem, and His name shall be Jesus (Matthew 1:21), the one they touched, held, and worshiped. John would write concerning Him: "That which was from the beginning, which we have heard, which we have seen with our eyes, which we looked upon and have touched with our hands" (1 John 1:1). Yes, we absolutely thank God for establishing eyewitness testimony, for bringing measurable, historical substance to our faith. However, one thing is worth more than a close-up look at the Son. It is God's promise about Him: *God clothed in flesh need not alarm.*

Despite the promise, we know that on page after page of the Bible, the people who see God fear Him. Isaiah saw His robe and trembled. When Peter watched Jesus fill the empty boat with large fish, he cried, "Depart from me, for I am a sinful man" (Luke 5:8). At the cross, one thief was shocked by the other's disrespect. "Don't you fear God?" (Luke 23:40). People who see God are aware of their own sin. They feel caught and exposed. They panic, and here's the point: Yes, God bares His holy arm—His only Son—to establish the apostles' eyewitness testimonies about Him and to stir in us the anticipated joy of seeing Him. But first, God reveals His Son to cast our sin upon Him.

A Lamb in whom no sin is found,
Yet bearing ours, He makes no sound
As He is lead to slaughter.

3 Our death upon the cross He died,
Yet see—this Lamb is living!
In Christ, we now stand justified,
His guiltlessness us giving!
Out of the anguish of His soul,
We have been cleansed, restored, made whole;
Baptized in Christ, made righteous!

Our Death upon the Cross He Died

The death and crucifixion of a man in Roman times is not memorable, certainly not a hundred generations later. But if He died *Our death upon the cross* and suffered our punishment, then His crucifixion is not simply one more among many. As unimaginable as being scourged and crucified are to us, the punishment Jesus endured encompassed more than the physical pain of a barbaric execution. Damnation is worse than death. Damnation is never ending. *Our death upon the cross He died* includes the absorption of the total and eternal wrath of God that was otherwise stored up for every person for every sin she or he ever committed throughout all of human history. The promise is tremendous. Is there proof? *Yet see—this Lamb is living!* There it is. Satan understood everything about the Lamb. That is why he tempted Him in the wilderness immediately after His Baptism. If Christ would have sinned, He could not be the acceptable sacrifice for us. God would have damned Him, He would still be dead, no one would have seen Him risen from the dead, and we would be awaiting the same just end measured in flames. "Alleluia!" introduces our Easter cry because the Lamb is living. It is our death upon the cross that He died, our punishment that He took. There is more.

Christ's death and resurrection are only half of salvation's equation. The other half—His guiltlessness—gives us access through heaven's door. Only holy, sinless, pure, perfect people enter paradise. In the mirror and all around us, we see only guilty people, not guilt*less*. A guiltless person has a spotless heart, where lust, laziness, greed, and grudge have left no stain. We do not really want God to peer into our hearts. We do not have what we need for salvation. Jesus gives it, but He could not give what He did not have.

Jesus established His guiltlessness by trusting His Father despite profound physical temptations after forty days without food in the wilderness. He established His guiltlessness by faithfully rebuking the chief priests and Pharisees, by warning His disciples, and by confronting those who denied their own sin. He established His guiltlessness by sacrificing sleep to compassionately heal those who were sick with disease and afflicted with disability. He established His guiltlessness by having mercy upon the demon-possessed and by graciously converting sinners who hated Him, such as Paul. By being the perfect Son, by honoring His father and His mother on earth, and by refusing to compromise the will of His Father in heaven, Jesus established His guiltlessness.

The guiltlessness Jesus established to become the sacrifice for us is what we need to be holy and pure and acceptable to God when His kingdom comes. How do we acquire this purity, this holiness of His? Paul answers repeatedly: "As many of you as were baptized into Christ have put on Christ" (Galatians 3:27) and "He saved us . . . by the washing of regeneration" (Titus 3:5) and "Christ loved the church and gave Himself up for her, that He might sanctify her, having cleansed her by the washing of water with the word" (Ephesians 5:25–26).

What about His death? How do we receive the benefit of it? It is the same baptismal answer; Paul could not have been clearer: "Do you not know that all of us who have been baptized into Christ Jesus were baptized into His death?" (Romans 6:3). Through Baptism, Jesus has given to you His death, His resurrection, His forgiveness, and His guiltlessness, and because He has given to you all of that, He has given to you His salvation.

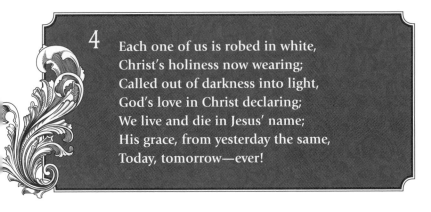

4 Each one of us is robed in white,
Christ's holiness now wearing;
Called out of darkness into light,
God's love in Christ declaring;
We live and die in Jesus' name;
His grace, from yesterday the same,
Today, tomorrow—ever!

Today, Tomorrow—Ever!

Forever is a power word and belongs to God alone. No one can steal or clone it. *Forever* is a key component of our congregation's 150th anniversary theme, "To God Be the Glory—Yesterday, Today, and Forever," so the author places the idea at the end of the center stanza. But then he replaces the word *glory* with *grace*. Why? God wants us to be in paradise forever, and He expresses His highest glory by giving it to us. We often associate glory with praise. Not so with God. God's glory is His work, not His praise. In John 12, Jesus said to Philip and Andrew, "The hour has come for the Son of Man to be glorified" (v. 23). He was not anticipating applause—He was forecasting His crucifixion. Jesus did not restore the sight of the man born blind (John 9) or call Lazarus back to life (John 11) to be praised. God's glory, above all, is His securing our salvation through Jesus' sacrificial work on the cross. He worked on behalf of the man born blind and on behalf of Lazarus and his sisters because He loved them, and in so doing, He previewed His greatest glory—His own death and rising and His giving us everlasting paradise—His grace.

God's grace and work to gain our eternal paradise is the key message of every miracle, person, and book in Scripture. The faithful works of the well-known Bible characters inspire us, but even more significant and beautifully consistent are the works of God. God forgives and saves. Being inspired is helpful; being redeemed is essential. Noah, Abraham, Moses, and David needed God's works. Noah walked with God, but there was that time with his wine (Genesis 9:21). Abraham's astonishing trust had him ready to put the knife to his son's neck (Genesis 22), but not before he had panicked, deceived, and exposed his wife to possible molestation (Genesis 20). Moses feared, loved, and trusted in God, not Pharaoh, but then disobeyed God when he refused to speak the word to the rock, striking it instead with his staff and then daring to take credit for the miraculous water spout at Meribah (Numbers 20:1–13). The number of battles King David won, relying completely upon the Lord to provide victory, is stunning. His foes included lions and bears and Goliath, the Geshurites, Amalekites, Benjaminites, Jebusites, Philistines, Ammonites, and Absalom. He prayed to God and trusted Him. However, we also remember His sin. He committed adultery with Bathsheba and murdered Uriah (2 Samuel 11). God brought Nathan to open David's eyes to the depth of his transgression. God's action, His word through Nathan, worked repentance in David's heart. "I have sinned against the LORD." Nathan declared immediately, "The LORD also has put away your sin" (12:13). David's subsequent prayer records the result of the Holy Spirit's work in his heart. "Have mercy on me, O God. . . . Wash me thoroughly from my iniquity, and cleanse me from my sin! . . . Hide Your face from my sins, and blot out all my iniquities. Create in me a clean heart, O God, and renew a right spirit within me. Cast me not away from Your presence, and take not Your Holy Spirit from me. Restore to me the joy of Your salvation, and uphold me with a willing spirit" (Psalm 51:1–2, 9–12).

The grace God gave to Noah, Abraham, Moses, and David is the same grace that He gives to us. In our hymn's first four stanzas, the author unfolds more than two dozen grace promises. He declares what God has done and is doing to make certain we are His forever. Take a moment to read the hymn again, line by line. Concentrate on and count God's promises and actions of grace for you.

> 5 Look to the heav'ns, lift up your eyes
> And understand this clearly:
> That this fair earth beneath those skies
> And all we love so dearly,
> Will one day face its fiery fate;
> Like smoke the heav'ns will dissipate
> At Jesus' reappearing!

Look to the Heavens,
Lift Up Your Eyes

All the stuff we love will burn. Peter believed it. "The heavens and earth are stored up for fire" (1 Peter 3:7). But isn't this an anniversary celebration hymn? What about praise? Why the harsh warning?

Are you listening? The hymn's author considered the world's drastic changes since our congregation's 1863 inception and the accelerated pace of culture's insistence upon changing the Third Petition of the Lord's Prayer from "Thy will" to "my will." The decades-old materialistic acquisition spree seems but one idolatrous option available today. When lies rush in, truth retreats. Our hearts hear the whispers: "You deserve it." "You worked for it." "You have the right." And we may hear ourselves humming, "My will be done on earth until I get to heaven."

Satan is concerned that his theme word, *my*, sounds selfish to children of God, so the master of camouflage goes to work rewording things. The deceiver's encouragement to live by the lie of "my will" often sounds like this: "Every choice you make to achieve happiness is a good one."

For the convenience of those who love them, idols are everywhere. Which is your favorite? Or do you prefer to spread your allegiance among several? Our Lord God does not want us to wander off. He did not post the Commandments in stone to keep us from what is delightful, but from what is harmful. It is impossible to sin without hurting ourselves, others, and our faith. Whoever prays this world's version of the Third Petition may succeed, even unintentionally, in suffocating his faith and trust in Jesus. What else could John have meant? "If anyone loves the world, the love of the Father is not in him" (1 John 2:15). Paul warns, "To set the mind on the flesh is death" (Romans 8:6).

Our idolatry will always be a problem. Willing rebellion against God did not begin recently. Eve was tantalized by the fruit of doubt. Adam, rather than faithfully leading his wife away from evil, was quick to participate. Now sinning comes naturally. Far from making an excuse for our selfish behavior, a biblical diagnosis of our spiritual hearts exposes the matter's seriousness. We have not, cannot, and will not keep God's will flawlessly, even when motivated by His love to do so. We have no excuse for loving ourselves and this world more than we love God. Most wonderfully, we do have a Savior. Imagining Jesus kneeling in the garden of Gethsemane brings calm because there Jesus vowed, "Not My will, but Yours, be done" (Luke 22:42).

How do we know that Jesus meant the petition He prayed? Meditating upon it resulted in bloody sweat. He then left the garden to consume for us the fires of Golgotha.

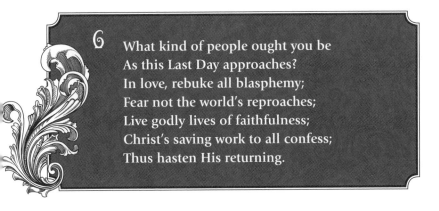

6 What kind of people ought you be
As this Last Day approaches?
In love, rebuke all blasphemy;
Fear not the world's reproaches;
Live godly lives of faithfulness;
Christ's saving work to all confess;
Thus hasten His returning.

In Love, Rebuke All Blasphemy

The Last Day is approaching. What are we going to do *before* it arrives? Drawing from Isaiah and Peter, the hymn's author sets down four verbs: *rebuke, fear not, live,* and *confess*. We will consider these verbs one at a time.

First, the hymn tells us that we rebuke blasphemy, not with condescension but with love for people. Feeling appalled because of the world's ways and the people who follow them or expressing disgust about it to one's like-thinking spouse or friend doesn't really count.

Today, a pronounced form of blasphemy is the constant drumming toward the normalizing of immoral and unnatural behavior. Ironically, people who attribute as much godly significance to consummating a marriage as they do to selecting a soft drink or checking social media also insist that fulfilling one's relational desire is of utmost importance to personal meaning. Be it premarital, extramarital, or pseudo-marital status, the blasphemer does what he wants.

Among God's highest gifts is not only creation but also creation's orderliness. To deny what is good and natural is, by default, to reject the One who did the ordering. So why does our culture insist upon doing so? In the pursuit of fulfillment, meaning, and pleasure, the blasphemer stiff-arms God's will and strokes his own. When God breathed the divine Spirit into Adam and brought Eve to him, He said of this husband and wife union, "It is good." God blessed marriage. Marriage is good and natural. In marriage children are born. The marriage meld is unique; the union of husband and wife in heart, body, and mind is formed in no other relationship. In marriage, we see a picture of the communion between Christ and His Bride, the Church. The assault against God's perfect design for life and humanity, in whatever form the attacks come, is blasphemy. It is willed stupidity. It is premeditated contempt for God's design. However and whenever God's ways for His children are thwarted, we must not commit sins of omission through silence and inactivity. We rebuke blasphemy with love for people.

What do I say if I am afraid? To rebuke is to confront, and we do not like to do that. We have been trained never to offend. We fear the kickback. Fear will actually keep us from lovingly confronting another even though our intent is to prevent earthly pain and potential eternal suffering. One step toward eliminating fear is recognizing that the Word we bring is not for the sake of binding up someone's life with Law, for restricting their movement and lifestyle against their desires and imagined freedom. The truth is, anyone committed to sinfulness is already bound, is without freedom, and has no control. We confront the blasphemer who lives in denial with the Word of Christ because He sets the sinner free (John 8:36) and gives life to the full (10:10).

Another step toward eliminating fear is to repent of the sin that it is. Fear swells because of our unwillingness or inability to believe God. Only decades ago, words such as *heaven* and *hell* had grip, even for those who were not showing up on Sunday mornings. Today's dismissal of eternal salvation and eternal damnation by much of the world and even by our own friends, co-workers, and family members and our fear of confronting them is like a time for God's people 2,700 years earlier. The Lord calls out through His prophet Isaiah:

> Lift up your eyes to the heavens, and look at the
> earth beneath; for the heavens vanish like smoke,

the earth will wear out like a garment, and those who dwell in it will die in like manner; but My salvation will be forever, and My righteousness will never be dismayed. . . . Fear not the reproach of man, nor be dismayed at their reviling. For the moth will eat them up like a garment, and the worm will eat them like wool, but My righteousness will be forever, and My salvation to all generations. (Isaiah 51:6–8)

It is very uncomfortable to hear that those who reject God's Word face a terrifying eternal finish. The world will end. Yet God's salvation will last forever. We get to tell this to others, and to do so, sometimes we need to rebuke with love. Live godly lives. That is this stanza's third directive. Rebuke, fear not, and live godly lives of faithfulness. When we live like we believe what we hear on Sundays, when our lives reflect Jesus' grace, patience, and sacrifice, others see and become more open to hearing about it.

One way to confess His saving work, the stanza's fourth directive, is to ask God to make your outlook more like Paul's. He said, "I am not ashamed of the gospel, for it is the power of God for salvation to everyone who believes" (Romans 1:16). You do not need to tell a soul that you are not ashamed of Christ. They will know when they hear you say things such as "God's forgiveness is amazing" or "What kind of power did it take for God to raise Jesus from the dead? I'm glad that we belong to Him!" or "We can't really imagine the pain of hell and the joy of heaven, but thank the Lord, He suffered the one and gives to us the other!"

7   Sing God the Father's majesty:
    Of naught He made creation!
    To God the Son all glory be:
    His blood wrought our salvation!
    The Holy Spirit magnify:
    He dwells within to sanctify—
    One God Most High forever!

His Blood Wrought Our Salvation

The first two words of the second line—*of naught*—encompass the universe and God's omnipotence. For emphasis, we teach our confirmands to say *ex nihilo*, the Latin rendering. "Out of nothing" is what the Bible's first verse is all about: "In the beginning, God created the heavens and the earth" (Genesis 1:1). And God is the subject of the verb *created*. Each additional time *create* appears in the Old Testament, God is the subject. Pyramids, moon landings, satellite stations, and organ transplants are on the first page of man's achievements. *Create* is not on the list. God, not man, creates out of nothing. "Nothing" is not much to work with when creation includes oceans, galaxies, oak trees, tulips, hummingbirds, black bears, and people.

Speaking of oceans, the Atlantic covers 41 million square miles. How many gallons is that? Speaking of galaxies, scientists measure outer space by the distance that light travels in one year, called a light year. Light particles travel 186,000 miles per second. We comprehend 60 or 70 miles per hour. God created light to move not a mere 1,000 miles per hour, but 186,000 miles every second. Light speed takes us around the earth 400 times in one minute, but to reach Alpha Centauri, the nearest star, takes five years. And imagine flying for 27,000 uninterrupted years at light speed, a smooth 669 million miles per hour, to reach the center of the Milky Way. That is a lot of acreage. There are billions of galaxies. Nearly 3,000 years ago, King David announced to the choirmaster, "The heavens declare the glory of God, and the sky above proclaims His handiwork" (Psalm 19:1).

Stacking creation facts to highlight the chasm between man and God risks minimizing God's insurmountable power. Describing an aspect or two of God's six-day project for a reader to ponder is one thing. It is another thing to create everything out of nothing by sheer will and vocal command, and to do so demonstrates unapproachable, unfathomable raw might. Perhaps we do better to humbly pray with the psalmist:

> When I look at Your heavens, the work of Your fingers, . . . what is man that You are mindful of him? (Psalm 8:3–4)

Why *does* God pay attention to us? Picturing God's hand cradling heaven's stars raises the question. At least it ought to. However, to pause here, as if the hymn stanza's purpose is to awaken awe in the presence of God's *of naught* power is to miss the more significant difference between us and God and the greater goal of this doxological concluding stanza. Returning to the psalmist's question, if one little man staring into the night sky is moved to ask, "What is man that You are mindful of him?" then the question that forms the moment he considers the inestimable contrast between his sinfulness and God's holiness must be "What is man that You do not smite him?"

Paul knows that apart from Christ, God should strike man down eternally (1 Corinthians 15:21). Recall that Paul did not say, "I decided to know nothing among you except the beauty of creation, for we preach Christ created!" No, that he did not say. Of course He believes that Jesus is the Creator (1 Corinthians 8:6; Colossians 1:15–16). However, Paul knew that the splendor of creation speaks for itself. It declares the majesty of the Creator (Psalm 19:1), but it says *nothing* about Christ the Redeemer! The mountains and stars cannot tell us why God would not damn us. Paul was "eager to preach the gospel . . . for it is the power of

God for salvation" (Romans 1:15–16), and he faced starvation, stoning, imprisonments, and death to do it. The answer to both questions—why is God mindful of us, and why does God not smite us—is as simple as John 3:16. God loves us and gave up His only Son for us. Paul captures both points with one verse: "We preach Christ crucified" (1 Corinthians 1:23).

Christ accomplished all, but without the Holy Spirit all He did would do us no good! The Holy Spirit finds us dead in sin, converts us to new life and faith in Christ, and keeps us in the one true faith using the only means God appointed—the Word of God, Holy Baptism, and the Holy Supper. With sheer joy, we sing once more the height of God's glory proclaimed by our closing stanza's center line: *His blood wrought our salvation!*

Stricken, Smitten, and Afflicted

1 Stricken, smitten, and afflicted,
See Him dying on the tree!
'Tis the Christ, by man rejected;
Yes, my soul, 'tis He, 'tis He!
'Tis the long-expected Prophet,
David's Son, yet David's Lord;
Proofs I see sufficient of it:
'Tis the true and faithful Word.

2 Tell me, ye who hear Him groaning,
Was there ever grief like His?
Friends through fear His cause disowning,
Foes insulting His distress;
Many hands were raised to wound Him,
None would intervene to save;
But the deepest stroke that pierced Him
Was the stroke that justice gave.

3 Ye who think of sin but lightly
Nor suppose the evil great
Here may view its nature rightly,
Here its guilt may estimate.
Mark the sacrifice appointed,
See who bears the awful load;
'Tis the Word, the Lord's anointed,
Son of Man and Son of God.

4 Here we have a firm foundation,
Here the refuge of the lost:
Christ, the Rock of our salvation,
Is the name of which we boast;
Lamb of God, for sinners wounded,
Sacrifice to cancel guilt!
None shall ever be confounded
Who on Him their hope have built.

LSB 451
TEXT: THOMAS KELLY (1769–1855)

his is a beautifully moving hymn. The melody is built on the repetition of two eighth notes followed by two quarter notes, two eighth notes and two more quarter notes, creating a pulsing, steady rhythm, causing the worshiper to sense the three beats per measure, or even to lightly tap the fingers or to keep time with one's foot. The melody, with the continual, steady three beats, helps me picture the steady journey of our Lord through His last days on earth, beginning with the donkey and palms and concluding with the guards, whips, and spear, and His last words. Before arriving at Golgotha, Jesus led His disciples to the Upper Room for the Passover Meal and the giving of the Lord's Supper. He continued to the garden and prayed in distress. My mind hears the melody and rhythm while seeing Jesus, through the words of the evangelists, push through the night—the courtyard, the rooster, Pilate, Herod, high priest, jeering crowds—He pushes on, taking strikes and facial blows, the scourge, and crossbeam, determined to trust His Father and do His will.

Each stanza pulls us to the cross for a different reason. The opening line captures Holy Week and the culmination of God's plan of salvation—the cross—through Isaiah's eighth-century BC vision. His fifty-third chapter, which is accented in Good Friday worship, is referenced by Matthew, Mark, Luke, and John in the Gospels, by Paul in his letters, and again by John in Revelation. The hymn's author pinpoints history's key event for God's baptized children by reciting three key words from Isaiah; the imagery is vivid: *stricken, smitten, and afflicted.*

Our reflection on stanza 1 asks the question, given the nature of the Jews and Greeks of Paul's day, none of whom were interested in a crucified Savior, if it is different today. Is anyone really interested in a stricken, smitten, crucified man?

Stanza 2 accentuates that the greatest injustice of all history is the very means by which God works out His justice to save us. The radical exchange, completely and totally unjust—our guilt and sin for Christ's pure heart and life—is remarkable, and it is the heart of the Christian message. We will turn to the story of Jehoshaphat in 2 Chronicles as well as to Isaiah to emphasize the absolute importance of justice to God Almighty, keying in on the phrase *But the deepest stroke that pierced Him Was the stroke that justice gave.*

How does the opening line of the third stanza meet you? It does not say, "If you think of sin but lightly." It does not say, "Those who think of sin but lightly." It is direct; it leaves no one excluded. *Ye who think of sin but lightly* means you and me. Obviously, unbelievers have little understanding of the severity of their sinful condition. But even we as children of God, instructed in faith yet children of wrath by nature, cannot fully comprehend what the word announces (Ephesians 2:3). The stanza gives reason to review the important difference between the actual sins we commit and the sin that dwells within us (the power of sin and our inherited, corrupt nature). *That* is the real problem—our nature. For the purpose of heightening our thanksgiving for the sacrifice Christ made, we will cite three examples of corrupt thought patterns that reside in us as a result of our nature. Also, the degradation of crucifixion, its dehumanizing impact, serves to increase our love and trust in Jesus and His Good Friday sacrifice for us when it is more deeply understood. Stanza 4 employs three metaphors—foundation, Rock, and Lamb—to complete the hymn's message of God's gift to us in the sacrifice of His only Son. Readings from the books of Job and 2 Samuel will help us absorb the significance of those metaphors before concluding with the reality, not a symbol or mere image, of our actual Savior, sacrificed of God. To Him we belong. There is no confusion. We are not confounded, for God has built our hope and faith in Christ, the *Sacrifice to cancel guilt.*

> 1 Stricken, smitten, and afflicted,
> See Him dying on the tree!
> 'Tis the Christ, by man rejected;
> Yes, my soul, 'tis He, 'tis He!
> 'Tis the long-expected Prophet,
> David's Son, yet David's Lord;
> Proofs I see sufficient of it:
> 'Tis the true and faithful Word.

See Him Dying on the Tree!

Remember what Paul said about Jews and Greeks? The former demand signs, and the latter demand wisdom. Paul insists that Christ crucified is a "stumbling block to Jews and folly to Gentiles" (1 Corinthians 1:23). Today's "Greeks" drive past church. They want proof. They want science. The rest of us, perhaps, are more like Paul's Jews. We like signs, dramatic ones. They stir emotions and break through our preoccupations. We do not need sea partings or Jordan River crossings (Exodus 14; Joshua 3), but the more impressive the sign, the better. Full parking lots, a massive pipe organ or an awesome praise band, an incredible youth pastor and preschool with a waiting list, a pastor who knows everyone by name, or a state of the art church app. None of these things is wrong, and some are helpful. The problem, again, in terms of proof and signs, is whether our desire for uplifting feelings, for a "great worship experience," has replaced our absolute reliance on receiving the one thing needful—Christ crucified (Luke 10:42).

It was evident to Paul and tragic: neither the Jews nor the Greeks were interested in a crucified Savior. Is it so different today? Is anyone really interested in *stricken, smitten, and afflicted*? What Isaiah reports is the same as what Matthew tells us. In Isaiah's account, there were speakers who at first believed that the Suffering

Servant was stricken and smitten by God because He was getting what He deserved, much the same as one may have less sympathy for a prison inmate serving a just sentence or for someone suffering pronounced health issues caused by irresponsible habits. Likewise, on Golgotha, there were those who believed Jesus was afflicted, nailed on the cross, for what He had done. They spoke out, saying God could rescue Him if Jesus desired since He claimed to be His Son (implying, of course, that He was *not* God's Son and was receiving what He deserved [Matthew 27:43]). Others were converted at the scene, eyes opened by the Holy Spirit. Not only the centurion, but "those who were with him . . . saw the earthquake and what took place, they were filled with awe and said, 'Truly this was the Son of God!'" (27:54). And the speakers in Isaiah, given eyes of faith, see the truth and interject, "But He was pierced for *our* transgressions" (Isaiah 53:5, emphasis added).

Today is Good Friday. This hymn's opening line takes us to God's culminating historical event through the preaching of Isaiah. What would be the means of generating forgiveness for the world, for all sinners of all time? Prior to unwrapping Calvary's scene and its significance for us (ch. 53), Isaiah was himself touched by God in an unforgettable and preparatory manner (ch. 6), through which God shaped his preaching and understanding of what matters most. In the holy temple, Isaiah encounters the presence of God seated upon a throne and flanked by six-winged angels. Isaiah is overcome and believes he is to be consumed by God's wrath. Using tongs, an angel touches a burning coal to Isaiah's lips, which at first must have felt like anything but salvation. What he felt was fire. And then the Word was spoken: "Your guilt is taken away, and your sin atoned for" (Isaiah 6:7).

The angel had come from the place of sacrifice and spoke the language of atonement using the Hebrew word for "forgive." Just as God uses baptismal water to bring forgiveness from the cross, the place where Christ was sacrificed for us, so the burning coal came from the altar, the place where the blood sacrifice of an animal was made, to cover the penalty for sin. In no way did Isaiah assist in the receiving of forgiveness by absorbing pain, but it is reasonable to suggest that the elements of a hot coal, tender lips, the altar, blood, and sacrifice all worked to heighten in his mind the seriousness of his sin and the extremes God would take in order to grant forgiveness. The hymnwriter, with three opening words, brings us to the heart of Isaiah's proclamation and to the only sign we need—the cross.

> We esteemed Him *stricken, smitten* by God, and
> *afflicted.* But He was pierced for our transgressions.
> (Isaiah 53:4–5, emphasis added)

2 Tell me, ye who hear Him groaning,
Was there ever grief like His?
Friends through fear His cause disowning,
Foes insulting His distress;
Many hands were raised to wound Him,
None would intervene to save;
But the deepest stroke that pierced Him
Was the stroke that justice gave.

The Stroke That Justice Gave

"Where's justice?" or "There ain't no justice!" and similar phrases are familiar but mean little if you have never met harsh, unfair treatment. Some nations victimize their own people. No one is moving to North Korea, Syria, or Venezuela. Some children, if they survive the womb, are mistreated or abused by their own parents. God vocalizes extreme displeasure with injustice. The name Jehoshaphat means "the Lord judges." When Jehoshaphat was king of Judah, he appointed judges:

> Consider what you do, for you judge not for man but for the LORD. He is with you in giving judgment. Now then, let the fear of the LORD be upon you. Be careful what you do, for there is no injustice with the LORD our God, or partiality or taking bribes. (2 Chronicles 19:6–7)

God is so serious about giving love, care, and fair treatment to others that He says, "Let the fear of the Lord be upon you," which means "let a terrifying sense of God's presence restrain you from any injustice" (*Concordia Self-Study Bible*, note on 2 Chronicles 19:7). It would be shortsighted and selfish for us to think that

God is no longer as concerned about justice as He once was. We, too, need to be concerned.

We have no precise measuring stick to gauge our stewardship and care for others. God does not expect us to give away every possession or to find suffering to endure when He has not brought it. But He does expect us to give time, energy, expertise, money—deliberate effort or even sacrifice—to help alleviate injustices endured by others. The reminder that from those to whom much has been given much is expected is from the Bible (Luke 12:48). Have we become too comfortable being comfortable? God speaks against those whose lives do not reflect the same love and care toward others—the same justice—as they themselves receive from God. The word *justice* occurs 425 times in the Old Testament. One of God's primary goals in the Book of Isaiah is to establish justice, and ultimately, for *Yahweh*, the goal of His justice is salvation (Lessing, 73). Even so, justice is also something for God's people to display, as proclaimed early on by Isaiah, "Learn to do good; seek justice, correct oppression; bring justice to the fatherless, plead the widow's cause" (1:17).

For those who *have* experienced injustice, great unfairness, mistreatment—perhaps you have a loved one who was unfairly dismissed from a job or perhaps your child is bullied—how comforting this stanza must be. The One who was truly innocent understands the mental anguish and torment of unjust persecution and of being convicted of crimes He did not commit. The hymn's author asks a good question. *Was there ever grief like His?* His friends left Him (Mark 14:50). There were not only hands raised to wound Him (Luke 22:63–65), but also no one intervened to save Him. He was taken away by oppression and without justice (Isaiah 53:8). They came after Him with clubs and swords as He finished praying (Matthew 26:36–56). The bogus back-and-forth trials with Pilate and Herod lingered all night. "He had done no violence and there was no deceit in His mouth" (Isaiah 53:9). But God made "Him to be sin who knew no sin, so that in Him we might become the righteousness of God" (2 Corinthians 5:21). "He was pierced for our transgressions; He was crushed for our iniquities" (Isaiah 53:5). And speaking of injustice, "All we like sheep have gone astray; we have turned—every one—to his own way; and the LORD has laid on Him the iniquity of us all" (v. 6).

Jesus knows about injustice. We call it "Good Friday." Good Friday means that the total, comprehensive injustice put upon Christ serves God's justice. God's justice is not vengeance toward sinners. God's justice is to make sure His vengeance is satisfied by His own Son, who took the punishment He did not deserve. Good Friday means that the punishment for our sin has been fully served and absorbed to fully secure the salvation of His children. Good Friday means *But the deepest stroke that pierced Him Was the stroke that justice gave.*

> 3   Ye who think of sin but lightly
> Nor suppose the evil great
> Here may view its nature rightly,
> Here its guilt may estimate.
> Mark the sacrifice appointed,
> See who bears the awful load;
> 'Tis the Word, the Lord's anointed,
> Son of Man and Son of God.

Ye Who Think of Sin But Lightly

I magine a man confessing, "Pastor, I committed adultery that resulted in a pregnancy, and I paid for the abortion." Imagine the pastor assuring him, "Jesus died an unselfish, terrible death to cover your guilt." But in this imagined story, the man does not say, "Thank you, Pastor. I need Jesus desperately. I can't believe what I did. I am so ashamed and feel so guilty. Lord, have mercy." Instead he says, "Pastor, there are Ten Commandments, right? I didn't do too well on two, but I'm pretty good on the other eight." Most of us are not like that. We don't think we're pretty good on eight. We think we're pretty good on all ten. Our human nature is so bent that we would succeed even without societal encouragement to *think of sin but lightly Nor suppose the evil great*.

Remember the difference between the individual sins you and I commit and the very essence of our fallen, depraved, inherited sinful nature? Paul uses the word *sin* both as a verb (as in Romans 3:23: "All have sinned and fall short") and as a noun (as in Romans 5:12: "Sin came into the world through one man"). The former refers to our actions, and the latter refers to sin as a power or disease, as the core of what we are and why we sin. Understanding the concept is as simple as understanding the oncologist who says, "There is a reason you have pain, feel sluggish, are losing weight, are always tired, and feel weak. Your body is filled with cancer." That is when one realizes that although the symptoms are not pleasant, the underlying condition is horrifying.

We commit individual sins. The origin of these sinful acts is our inner darkness, our inherited nature, and it results in a ghastly consequence: we are "catastrophically separated from the eternal love of God" (Rutledge, 174). We are ripe for damnation at the moment of our conception, and our nature establishes ingrained sinful patterns. A first example: What comes naturally for us is to desire that whatever happens is for our own advantage. We try to think of others first and not worry about ourselves (Philippians 2:3–4), but who succeeds?

A second example: We have an insatiable appetite for idols. Regarding the First Commandment, "You shall have no other gods," very few Christians are tempted to turn away from Jesus to worship Allah. We are thankful that Jesus won salvation for us. However, regarding the additional intangible benefits of identity, meaning, satisfaction, and security that also come from the cross through Baptism, these we may attempt to squeeze out of the tangible, such as a 401(k), condos, cars, and clothing. We lust after emotional peace "in a consumerist culture by using the material world in order to pamper the inner self" (Kolb and Arand, 87).

A third example: We desire someone else's approval over God's. Many of us want to matter, to be heroic; we need to justify ourselves to others because we believe our worth is measured by our own achievement. Some people seek approval through appearance or simply by being nice or by being a faithful employee. How corrupt, how controlling is the sin that dwells within us when we are unable to work, serve, strive, and help simply out of thanksgiving to God for what He accomplished for us on Good Friday. What He did for us on the cross proves our worth to Him and eliminates our need to justify ourselves to others. And let's look more closely at what He did. Jesus would not die with a swift beheading, grotesque though it is. The degradation and shame of crucifixion is so horrible that it was an offense against good manners for respectable people to speak of this hideous death. Further, the indignity of crucifixion "must call forth a concept of sin that is large enough to match it" (Rutledge, 200) Understanding the detestable nature of crucifixion underscores the severity of our fallen, lost condition, how much we are worth to God, and also provides immeasurable incentive to resist any urge to use our achievements or anything else to prop ourselves up before God and neighbor.

We may think lightly of sin. God does not. He never has. Nor does He neglect to estimate our guilt; rather He calculates it precisely. Out of His love and mercy, He planned the necessary, wretched, dehumanizing crucifixion. Out of His love and mercy, He sent the only One who could bear *the awful load; . . . the Lord's anointed, Son of Man and Son of God.*

4   Here we have a firm foundation,
    Here the refuge of the lost:
    Christ, the Rock of our salvation,
    Is the name of which we boast;
    Lamb of God, for sinners wounded,
    Sacrifice to cancel guilt!
    None shall ever be confounded
    Who on Him their hope have built.

Here We Have a Firm Foundation

Unlike the preceding stanzas in this hymn, stanza 4 bypasses any description of our problems and opens immediately with the solution, our *firm foundation.* When our young children become deathly sick or when our adult children turn away from Christ, when our minds are blurred by emotional pain, we need assurance that our life's foundation has not cracked. We need the firm foundation of God's Word, His Son, the cross, the empty tomb, and His resurrection.

My good friend was a project foreman for bridge construction in northern Minnesota. When I asked what holds up the massive concrete bridge pillars, he explained that piles—steel I-beams— serve as the foundation for the pillars. The piles are set vertically thirty-six inches apart. Next, a ten-ton hydraulic hammer, eight feet tall and twelve inches in diameter, drives the piles into the ground until they are deep enough. How deep is enough? My friend said, "When the hammer slams down ten times and the pile moves down less than an inch, that's deep enough for a firm bridge foundation."

It turns out that my friend needed and had a foundation that was much stronger than bridge pilings. Cancer came. No doubt it has struck someone you know. When it comes, though, we claim our foundation with Job. God let Satan take Job's wife, seven sons, three daughters, all his possessions, and his good health. When he was about to crack, teetering between depression and hopelessness, God assured him, with a series of sharp questions spanning over four chapters (Job 38–41), that when all earthly evidence suggests otherwise, he can trust the Lord. One of the questions God asks Job is this:

> Where were you when I laid the foundation of the earth? (Job 38:4)

My friend built bridge foundations. Long before man was building such pathways, God laid the foundation of the earth. That, of course, is figurative language. God laid the foundation of the earth by His incomprehensible will, by the immeasurable power of His Word. He created the earth out of nothing. He holds it in orbit with its moon. By His will, He sustains in space the sun and all stars. Our foundation is the Creator of all foundations, "the Maker of heaven and earth."

CHRIST, THE ROCK

Ultimately, our foundation is *Christ, the Rock* of our salvation. We may call upon Him as swiftly as King David, who sends a rapid fire of acclamations to the Lord after having faced death, battles, and spears. One can sense his emotion, thanksgiving, joy, and relief in this song on the day the Lord delivered him from his enemies. See the number of times David says "my" and the vivid titles he attributes to His Lord, all describing His dominance, His impenetrable and protective nature, upon which David relied.

> The LORD is my rock and my fortress and my deliverer, my God, my rock, in whom I take refuge, my shield, and the horn of my salvation, my stronghold and my refuge, my savior; You save me from violence. I call upon the LORD, who is worthy to be praised, and I am saved from my enemies. (2 Samuel 22:2–4)

THE NAME OF WHICH WE BOAST

Sometimes upon rescue, with relief and joy, we sing with David: "The LORD is my rock, my shield, my savior." Other times, even when met with earthly defeat, perhaps especially then, we may still boast in the Lord. Jeremiah did. "But let him who boasts boast in this, that he understands and knows Me, that I am the LORD who practices steadfast love" (Jeremiah 9:24). The psalmist said, "My soul makes its boast in the LORD" (Psalm 34:2) continually because God saved him from his foes (44:7–8), and Paul urges us to boast in the Lord alone (Romans 15:17; 1 Corinthians 1:31; 2 Corinthians 10:17; Galatians 6:14).

Here it is, Good Friday, and this devotion has focused on earthly trials. When there is pain and death, yes, the Lord is our foundation in all times of need. But the melody reaches its high point with this phrase:

Lamb of God, for sinners wounded, Sacrifice to cancel guilt!

Here is our reason to boast, above all others—the Lord was wounded, fatally, with scourge, spear, and nail because of our sin, by His own Father, to cover it, all of our guilt. Brought to faith, we boast in Christ, not in metaphors of foundation, rock, or lamb, but in the reality of Good Friday. Christ, the Son of God, was sacrificed for us. To Him we belong. There is no confusion, for God has built our hope and faith in Christ, the *Sacrifice to cancel guilt!*

If Christ Had Not Been Raised from Death

1 If Christ had not been raised from death
Our faith would be in vain,
Our preaching but a waste of breath,
Our sin and guilt remain.
But now the Lord is ris'n indeed;
He rules in earth and heav'n:
His Gospel meets a world of need—
In Christ we are forgiv'n.

2 If Christ still lay within the tomb
Then death would be the end,
And we should face our final doom
With neither guide nor friend.
But now the Savior is raised up,
So when a Christian dies
We mourn, yet look to God in hope—
In Christ the saints arise!

3 If Christ had not been truly raised
His Church would live a lie;
His name should nevermore be praised,
His words deserve to die.
But now our great Redeemer lives;
Through Him we are restored;
His Word endures, His Church revives
In Christ, our risen Lord.

LSB 486
TEXT: CHRISTOPHER M. IDLE, B. 1938; © 1985 THE JUBILATE GROUP
(ADMIN. HOPE PUBLISHING CO., CAROL STREAM, IL 60188). ALL
RIGHTS RESERVED. USED BY PERMISSION.

ome of Paul's people in Corinth had taken such a huge step away from the Christian faith; one might think he was writing to unbelievers. "How can some of you say that there is no resurrection of the dead?" (1 Corinthians 15:12). What they had done is settle into the skeptical and unbelieving patterns of the day, even to the degree of denying the Easter triumph of the Lord's physical resurrection from the dead. Hearing that Christ is risen brought little relief to those whose opinion about resurrection was formed long before Paul showed up. Homer, Pliny the Elder, and other ancient philosophers and poets laughed at the thought of resurrection. Death does not back up. It does not work in reverse. Deteriorating flesh is not revived. The logical mind-set was deeply embedded in society. When early Christians stepped out of their house churches, they entered the land of people who denied their central claim. The message "Christ is risen!" was completely contradictory to what the people knew to be true. There is no resurrection of the dead! Once a person goes the way of death, there is no coming back (Wright, 32–35).

This hymn follows Paul's outline in 1 Corinthians 15:12–28, where he sets up a series of if-then statements to show the repercussions of denying the testimony of the women at the tomb and of the apostles and of others to whom Jesus appeared after His resurrection. Paul squarely addresses the error by spelling out the impact it makes upon the collective blessings of faith. If Christ is not risen, we are stuck with our sin, death rules, and damnation awaits us.

Frankly, I have never met a church member who didn't believe Christ rose. I have met a handful who *left* the church because they no longer believed it, but we Christians know and believe that Christ's resurrection is the bedrock of our faith. While Paul needed to convince the people of Corinth of the Gospel's resurrection truth, the blessing for us in 1 Corinthians 15 and this hymn is both a strengthening of our certainty that Christ is literally, physically risen and a deepening of our understanding of how vital Christ's resurrection is for the securing of all the gifts

He wants to give, including our resurrection, changing also our mortal state to immortal from corruptible to incorruptible.

Following Paul's if-then pattern of argumentation in the face of skepticism in 1 Corinthians 15, the hymn's author establishes a clear outline and repeats it in each stanza. It looks like this:

> *If Christ* . . . is not raised,
> *Then* . . . something bad.
> *But* . . . Christ is risen,
> *Therefore* . . . something good.

The outline is simple and is used for each stanza. The three stanzas relate to one another, each with its own nuance regarding the horrific negative circumstance we face if Christ is not risen and the joyous, triumphant reality that is ours because Christ is risen.

Stanza 1 ties Christ's resurrection to forgiveness; if Christ had not been raised, then our sin and guilt would remain. But because Christ is raised, preaching is not *a waste of breath,* and His Gospel truth meets our ultimate need—*in Christ we are forgiv'n.* Stanza 2 clarifies a second harsh, inescapable reality apart from Christ's resurrection: if Christ still lay within the tomb, death is the end for us too. But because He is raised up, when a Christian dies, we mourn and look to God in hope. Stanza 3 exposes the ludicrous nature of faith if Christ is not risen and points to the restored, eternal life we have in Christ because He is truly raised.

Here are a couple of noticeable and helpful things about the hymn's tune. In everyday speak, it is upbeat and uplifting. The opening musical line repeats almost exactly in the second. Together, these two musical lines make up the first half of each stanza. Two four-note descending musical phrases form the heart of this portion of the melody. Look at the first four notes and then at the next four. Listen to them or hum them. How does a composer create an uplifting melody that also captures the contrast in each stanza, the frightening first half of each stanza with the wonderful truth and sure hope in each stanza's second half? Two short descending musical phrases match up with the meaning of the if-then sobering descriptions in each stanza.

The musical high point of the melody is assigned to the stanza's message of triumph, which begins with *But now.* Three times we sing the strong, uplifting, and joyful phrase: *But now the Lord is ris'n indeed* (st. 1); *But now the Savior is raised up* (st. 2); and *But now our great Redeemer lives* (st. 3).

Our congregation loves this hymn, and it did not take long to establish that fact. Children like the melody and understand the words. Parents and grandparents sing with full voice, families frequently request it for a funeral, and it is always a welcome component of our Easter worship. If you are familiar with the hymn, I'm sure you share our appreciation. If not, then may you look forward to learning it.

> 1   If Christ had not been raised from death
>   Our faith would be in vain,
>   Our preaching but a waste of breath,
>   Our sin and guilt remain.
>   But now the Lord is ris'n indeed;
>   He rules in earth and heav'n:
>   His Gospel meets a world of need—
>   In Christ we are forgiv'n.

But Now the Lord Is Ris'n Indeed

"How can some of you say that there is no resurrection of the dead?" (1 Corinthians 15:12). If Paul had been debating with the unbelievers of Corinth, the question would make more sense. But he is writing to his own converts who were influenced by the prevailing viewpoint of the day that once a person passes into death, he is never coming back. To these people, the notion of a corpse coming back to life was grotesque. Talking to them about Christ's rising would be like my talking to you about elephants flying.

Homer, the eighth-century-BC poet, who was perhaps as influential in the Greek world as Scripture is to Christians, flat-out denied the resurrection of the dead. In an oft-quoted line from his *Iliad*, the character Achilles tells Priam: "Lamenting for your son will do no good at all. You will be dead yourself before you bring him back to life." Another poet has Apollo testifying, "Once a man has died, and the dust has soaked up his blood, there is no resurrection." Many people in the ancient world had etched onto their tombstones this epitaph: "I was not, I was, I am not, I don't care." These examples from N. T. Wright's work *The Resurrection of the Son of God* (32–34) help us to understand why some of Paul's converts had regressed to the point of denying Christianity's central claim.

Evidently, those Christians may have believed that after death they would live spiritually but not physically. Paul calls out the serious ramifications of their error in 1 Corinthians 15:12–19, and this hymn's author takes note. *If Christ had not been raised from death*, then as a damning matter of fact, *Our sin and guilt remain!* Even if eternal life were only spiritual, it still would not be granted to anyone because if Christ had not been raised, with sin and guilt running us through, there would be for us no escaping His wrath. The fact is we will be raised to a physical eternal life that is not merely a do-over of our mortal bodies with their present weaknesses and limitations. Our bodies will be raised to a glorified, incorruptible state in keeping with Christ's resurrected body (Philippians 3:21).

Praise be to God, our sin and guilt do not remain, as Christ's resurrection validates the sacrificial nature of His crucifixion. His was not one more dehumanizing and forgotten barbaric execution among hundreds or thousands. His crucifixion is unlike all others because it accounts for the sins of the world—and His resurrection confirms it.

However, just because we need the resurrection of Christ does not mean that He rose, any more than saying, "I need a new car to get to work," means that one will appear in the driveway. Listen for Paul's key phrase twice repeated:

> I would remind you, brothers, of the gospel I
> preached to you . . . by which you are being saved.
> . . . For I delivered to you as of first importance
> what I also received: that Christ died for our sins
> in accordance with the Scriptures, that He was bur-
> ied, that He was raised on the third day in accor-
> dance with the Scriptures. (1 Corinthians 15:1–4)

The Old Testament speaks prophetically and emphatically in isolated verses and chapters about the coming of Christ together with His crucifixion and resurrection. One thinks of Isaiah 53;

Psalm 22; and Daniel 12:2: "Those who sleep in the dust of the earth shall awake, some to everlasting life, and some to shame and everlasting contempt." For Paul, however, "in accordance with the Scriptures" does not refer only to isolated texts, powerful and true though they are! It means the entire Old Testament thrust, the entire gravitation, from God's promise to crush Satan's head (Genesis 3:15) through John the Baptist's culminating proclamation (John 1:29), is driving toward the merciful crucifixion of Jesus and His almighty and glorious resurrection.

In essence, Paul is saying, "If you think I am lying about Christ's rising, you must accuse the Old Testament writers and God Himself of lying because, in accordance with the Scriptures, Christ would die and rise for the forgiveness and salvation of all who repent and believe."

We need Christ risen. In fact, He has been raised from the dead. *His Gospel meets a world of need—In Christ we are forgiv'n.*

2 If Christ still lay within the tomb
Then death would be the end,
And we should face our final doom
With neither guide nor friend.
But now the Savior is raised up,
So when a Christian dies
We mourn, yet look to God in hope—
In Christ the saints arise!

If Christ Still Lay within the Tomb

The second stanza of our devotional hymn brings the second *if*, and a subtle shift from *if Christ had not been raised* (st. 1) to *if Christ still lay within the tomb* (st. 2). On the one hand, the phrases are interchangeable. On the other, the emphasis is distinctly different within the context of each stanza. Stanza 1, as we have read, emphasizes *sin* and how there would be no forgiveness if Christ had not been raised. Stanza 2 emphasizes *death* and its looming consequences *If Christ still lay within the tomb*.

LOOMING CONSEQUENCE NUMBER 1: NO PURPOSE

If Christ remained dead, *Then death would be the end*, and if it were, what would be the point of life? As difficult as it is to fend off our sinful, selfish desires, even though we know that the Lord is going to return for us and will usher in a new heaven and a new earth (Revelation 21:1), if death is the end, then why not get what we can for as long as we can? Why not live for yourself? In many ways, isn't this how the world functions anyway? It is a logical way to live for anyone who believes that death is the end.

But death is not our end, not by an eternity, and our purpose is not shallow (Ephesians 5:2).

Looming Consequence Number 2: The Fog of Fear

Even if a person lives for the good of every man, woman, and child, if Christ still lay within the tomb, then she or he lives each day in the fog of the fear of death. Christians know that death may be physically painful. Death looms closer every day—we face our own death or that of one we love. The nonbeliever can only suppress reality to face the fog of fear each day. We know that we face our final doom with our Guide and Friend because He left the tomb!

Looming Consequence Number 3: The Emotional Pain of Death

A few years ago, a young couple from our congregation lost their little boy. An extremely aggressive infection, out of nowhere, brought him to unconsciousness and to death in less than forty-eight hours. He was to turn five. Their pain lingers but *If Christ still lay within the tomb Then death would be the end*, and their pain would never end. *But now the Savior is raised up!* Yet how do we know that His being raised up means we will also be raised up? Why should any parents who have lost a child believe they will see him or her again? Paul says in 1 Corinthians 15:22–23:

> For as in Adam all die, so also in Christ shall all be made alive. But each in his own order: Christ the firstfruits, then at His coming those who belong to Christ.

Just as we are connected to Adam by birth and have received from him our diseased, sinful nature, so are we connected to Jesus by rebirth—Baptism—and receive from Him resurrection and life everlasting. "Christ the firstfruits" is our evidence.

Firstfruits? Picture an apple tree, full bloom, apples hanging, poles propping up the branches, and then it happens—in the midst of hundreds of apples, the first one falls, the firstfruits. Soon they will all begin to fall. Jesus didn't fall. He rose, the first-fruits, the first of many. In rising, He defeated death for Himself and for us all.

We Mourn, Yet Look to God in Hope

Of course we mourn when we lose someone we love. It hurts. Easter triumph does not prevent pain in times of loss. The difference is that when we grieve, we do so with hope, sure hope, guaranteed hope. Paul promises, "The last enemy to be destroyed is death" (1 Corinthians 15:26) and more:

> We do not want you to be uninformed, brothers, about those who are asleep, that you may not grieve as others do who have no hope. For since we believe that Jesus died and rose again, even so, through Jesus, God will bring with Him those who have fallen asleep. . . . For the Lord Himself will descend from heaven with a cry of command, with the voice of an archangel, and with the sound of the trumpet of God. And the dead in Christ will rise first. (1 Thessalonians 4:13–16)

In Christ the saints arise!

3   If Christ had not been truly raised
His Church would live a lie;
His name should nevermore be praised,
His words deserve to die.
But now our great Redeemer lives;
Through Him we are restored;
His Word endures, His Church revives
In Christ, our risen Lord.

But Now Our Great Redeemer Lives

If Christ had not been raised, we would live *many* lies. Christ died to forgive us, He rose to conquer death, He ascended in glory, He is preparing a place for us, He will come again for us, and He will usher in His eternal kingdom—true, all true! But if Christ had *not* been raised from the dead—lies and more lies! We would be fooling ourselves, awaiting eternal judgment. If Christ were not raised, if He were still in the tomb, it could only mean that He would have stood under the crosshairs of judgment and been found guilty on account of His own sin, not on account of our sin. The triumph of Easter means that Jesus passed through judgment for us, a critical aspect of His saving work worthy of our praise, an aspect we sometimes gloss over. If Jesus would not have stood under judgment for us, when the time for our judgment comes, we would stand alone (Hebrews 9:27). Because He is risen, we can know that He went through judgment for us and will take us through it into paradise.

This hymn stanza with key words—*now, lives, restored, endures, revives*—points to the joyous aspect of the Lord's return. However, before we truly live and reign with the Lord in the new heavens and new earth, there is the matter of God's judgment. Christ's resurrection brings great comfort to this part of the sequence of our entering into the kingdom of God.

Horace Hummel was an amazing Old Testament St. Louis seminary professor who with a guttural, passionate, raspy voice would assert, "There can be no *salvation* if there is no *damnation!*" This means that God did not sacrifice His Son to save us from nothing. If there is no judgment and no wrath, then the Father would not have needed to point His Son toward Holy Week. He could have allowed Him to live a long, full life and die peacefully, without having run up against Pilate, the scourge, and cross, and then raised Him in order to conquer death. However, in order to strip away the fear of judgment and threat of eternal damnation, someone needed to go through Judgment Day for us and to suffer death and damnation in our place. Jesus, the Innocent One, was judged guilty for your sin and was crushed by His Father's wrath (Isaiah 53:5). Then He was raised to life because in Him there is no sin (1 John 3:5).

We hear the word *end* five times in Ezekiel 7:1–6. Here is a thought from Dr. Hummel taken from his discussion on Ezekiel (*Ezekiel 1–20*, 225–27):

> The human tendency is to embrace one-sidedly God's promises of salvation for those who believe, while disregarding God's threat of judgment upon those who do not believe—and to glibly assume, without self-examination, that the divine judgment certainly cannot apply to oneself. (226)

So true. We are more comfortable believing that God will *save us* than that He will *damn others*. It is not a pleasant thought. How can it be? God's Word says that the Last Day is coming. "Now the end is upon you, and I will send My anger upon you; . . . I will punish you for all your abominations. And My eye will not spare you nor will I have pity. . . . Now I will soon pour out My wrath upon you" (Ezekiel 7:3–4, 8). And yet we get a little lackadaisical with our confession of sins, as if it were impossible for us to fall away (1 Corinthians 10:12).

Jesus is so good to us. He even stood under judgment for our inability to properly repent. Judgment is coming, but Jesus is truly raised. We do *not* live a lie. Jesus went through Judgment Day for us. And because He is truly raised, we know that He is truly innocent. His innocence and holiness are His gifts to us, His baptized brothers and sisters. And when He returns, "We shall all be changed, in a moment, in the twinkling of an eye" (1 Corinthians 15:51–52). In an undetectable span of time, the Lord will change us from mortal to immortal, from perishable to imperishable. He is our risen Lord. In Him we are restored! Let the loud trumpet sound!

The Lord's My Shepherd, I'll Not Want

1 The Lord's my shepherd, I'll not want;
He makes me down to lie
In pastures green; He leadeth me
The quiet waters by.

2 My soul He doth restore again
And me to walk doth make
Within the paths of righteousness,
E'en for His own name's sake.

3 Yea, though I walk in death's dark vale,
Yet will I fear no ill;
For Thou art with me, and Thy rod
And staff me comfort still.

4 My table Thou hast furnishèd
  In presence of my foes;
  My head Thou dost with oil anoint,
  And my cup overflows.

5 Goodness and mercy all my life
  Shall surely follow me;
  And in God's house forevermore
  My dwelling place shall be.

LSB 710
TEXT: *THE PSALMS OF DAVID IN METER*, EDINBURGH, 1650

magine that I am standing next to you on the edge of the Going-to-the-Sun Road as we look out across a massive rocky and forested canyon at majestic Glacier National Park. What could I possibly say to enhance the moment? That is what it feels like now—what am I to say about the Twenty-Third Psalm? Perhaps comparing the ancient psalm to Luke's poetic account of Christ's birth is helpful. Learning about the shepherds that night who received from an angel the Good News, "Fear not. . . . Unto you is born . . . a Savior" (2:10–11), brings to us comfort and joy. Similarly, Psalm 23, with the Shepherd imagery and the Shepherd's sevenfold action—

> He makes me lie down
> He leads me beside still waters
> He restores my soul
> He leads me in paths of righteousness
> You are with me
> You prepare a table for me
> You anoint my head with oil—

brings comfort and peace, does it not? Try it. If I may suggest with all seriousness, sit with the psalm when you first awake, after each meal, and again at bedtime. Slow your mind. Ponder each phrase to absorb the message. Try it for seven days.

Without first reading a book about a shepherd's life and work, few of us comprehend it, and thus we cannot fully appreciate the psalm's imagery. Nonetheless, many of us gladly memorized the psalm. We turn to it especially when grief or anxiety overwhelm. The psalm's Gospel message appeals to both the mind and heart.

Turn to the psalm now. Look at the second word of the first verse, and the second-last word of the last verse. *Lord* is our oft-used English way of conveying the great name *Yahweh*. The psalm is comforting because it begins and ends with *Yahweh*; there is no god like Him (1 Samuel 2:2). *Yahweh* is steadfast in love (Psalm 118:1). He is gracious and merciful (Psalm 145:8). *Yahweh* keeps promises. He does mighty deeds (Psalm 77:11–20). He does for His sheep, for His children, what He says because He loves us. *Yahweh* is never a no-show. He does not miss. The center verses prescribe His acts; the outer mark them for completion, because His name is assigned to them.

David is clear. The Lord *is* his Shepherd. The verb is powerful. Not "if only" the Lord were my Shepherd, or "one cannot ever know for sure" if the Lord is our Shepherd, or "it all depends upon whether I choose" the Lord, or "I am too weak, too sinful, and too uncommitted" for the Lord to be my Shepherd. No, those are not correct. David did not say those things. David states the God-blessed reality, which is current and ongoing. David confesses, "The Lord *is* my shepherd" (Psalm 23:1, emphasis added). What is true for David, the Holy Spirit has made true for you and for me. Holy Baptism makes it so. The Holy Spirit leads us to say what is so true (1 Corinthians 12:3). Jesus *is* Lord. The Lord *is* our Shepherd.

Children of God who hear "The Lord is my Shepherd" often have two pictures in mind. There is the portrayal of Jesus the Good Shepherd leading the sheep, carrying the little lamb in His arms. There is also the Good Shepherd who "lays down His life for the sheep" (John 10:11), who carried His cross that none of those sheep given to Him by the Father would be lost (John 6:39), who carried His cross to account and atone for all sin (1 John 2:2), and to make certain that He Himself who would go through death could then take us through the dark valley (John 11:25–26; Romans 6:5). The Good Shepherd has the authority to lay down His life and to take it up again (John 10:18), and He does so (John 19:30; Mark 16:6; Matthew 28:6), thereby securing for all His baptized children via the power of the resurrection the psalm's final promise, to "dwell in the house of the Lord forever."

Turning to the hymn, one is touched by the poet's skill. Numerous times we hear in the second place what we expect to hear in the first place and vice versa. The technique invites concentration and adds to the hymn's beauty. Here is one simple example. We do not sing the straight-forward ESV translation, "He makes me lie down in green pastures" (23:2). The poet offers, *He makes me down to lie In pastures green.*

Points we will note in the devotions include the relationship between our want for the earthly material against the backdrop of knowing that the Shepherd gives us far more, even His life (st. 1). The second stanza raises the question of what it means to walk *within* the paths of righteousness, as opposed to *on* them. A quote from Luther supplements the third devotion. In the fourth devotion, we are reminded that the shepherding language is imagery. Further, as reassuring as Psalm 23:5 is, we consider what it means for the many Christians around the world whose cups are not overflowing. In the fifth stanza, we sing Psalm 23:6, one of the most beautiful and comforting passages in all of Scripture. Part of what makes it so is the Shepherd's name.

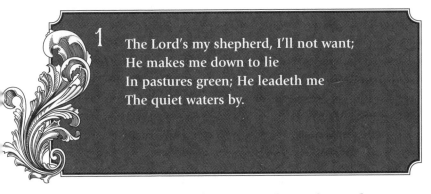

1
The Lord's my shepherd, I'll not want;
He makes me down to lie
In pastures green; He leadeth me
The quiet waters by.

The Lord's My Shepherd, I'll Not Want

The young shepherd walks in front of his sheep. David does not drive them; he calls them by name. Danger intensifies each evening with the cover of darkness shading the rocks, crags, and predators—beast or bandit. The shepherd keeps watch. He guards the sheep, and they know it. David's early life is simple, framed by God's provision in open country and His Word within his heart. The comforts his seven brothers enjoyed—roof, table, and family—were unfamiliar to David the shepherd. Nonetheless, he was content. God met his needs, leading him to the green pastures and refreshing waters enjoyed by his sheep. Consider this bit of commentary, dating to the late-nineteenth century:

> It would be well for us, amid the complexity and anxiety of our modern life, if we could catch something of his spirit. For the most part, our distress, our poverty, our carking care come, not from the smallness of our provisions, but from the largeness of our pampered desires. We are afraid that we shall not always have cake, and so we forget that God has promised that His children shall not lack bread. (Van Dyke, 33)

As spot-on as this is for my generation—we grew up when material things were coveted—materialism in the form of cars and clothes may not be the primary idol and source of envy for today's younger people, married with double incomes or not, as they readily afford whatever they want. What they want, they go get, often without waiting. That is not necessarily sinful. However, when wanting included waiting and saving, the illusion of contentment-about-to-be-fulfilled was sustained for as long as it took to collect the funds to make the acquisition. Acquiring, however, pulls back the curtain to let-down—anticipation is replaced by acquisition—and a new round of contentment-seeking begins. With means to bypass *wanting and waiting*, the sinful nature seeks contentment and fulfillment elsewhere and often does so through children and their achievements. Either way, contentment through acquisition or through achievement, the author's conclusion is helpful:

> A little plain living would lead to higher think-
> ing. It would do us good, it would do our children
> good, if we should learn that the real necessities
> and the best joys of human life are very simple . . .
> and for these we have a right always to trust God.
> (Van Dyke, 33)

For me, these words—*real necessities, best joys . . . are very simple, and for these we have a right always to trust God*—recently hit home. On my way home after a trip to Green Bay to play golf at a course I enjoy, I saw my wife a quarter mile from our driveway, alongside a brown-topped cattail marshy area. When she walked into the house, I asked, "So what were you doing?" My farm-girl bride replied, "Relocating a few toads from our window well to a habitat more to their liking." I had to wonder if my walk that afternoon, including the cost, was as satisfying as hers. For those moments of discontent when wanting becomes the dominant emotion against a perceived lack of worldly pleasure, we do well to ask: Why does the Maker of heaven and earth, the judge of all mankind, deal so lovingly with me?

The author whose thoughts about this psalm, which we were pleased to include above, also missed something: How does one sing or recite Psalm 23:1, "The LORD is my shepherd; I shall not want," without thinking about the words of the Good Shepherd as John recorded them? With the Lord as our Shepherd, surely we may enjoy contentment. Why waste life by wanting? But the Good Shepherd will do more. He will lay down His life for His sheep. The ease these days of finding even in small-town America a little boy or girl without loving, caring parents who are the Shepherd's instruments of provision accentuates the significance of looking past what the eyes *see*. So let us listen to what the voice of the Good Shepherd *says*. "I am the good shepherd. . . . I lay down My life for the sheep. . . . My sheep hear My voice, and I know them, and they follow Me. I give them eternal life, and they will never perish, and no one will snatch them out of My hand" (John 10:14–15, 27–28).

The Lord's my shepherd, I'll not want.

> 2   My soul He doth restore again
>   And me to walk doth make
>   Within the paths of righteousness,
>   E'en for His own name's sake.

My Soul He Doth Restore Again

here are seven beautiful things the Shepherd does for His sheep. The third in David's song of praise—*My soul He doth restore*—is it the result of the first two? *He makes me down to lie In pastures green, He leadeth me The quiet waters by*, and thus by His abundant providing and blessing He restores my soul? Or is His restoring my soul one more singular blessing and joy? And *My soul He doth restore again* means what exactly? Without delving into a complex Hebrew word study on *soul*, a word used more than seven hundred times in the Old Testament, the psalmists like to use the word to mean one's life, or one's self, or at risk of oversimplifying: *me*. "He restores me" does not have the poetic beauty of *My soul He doth restore again*, but the point I am making is that David is probably not referring to his soul only, a thing apart from his body. When the Lord provides earthly joys—good rest, a beautiful morning's walk, food, family, love, and fresh air—the receiving of His gifts stirs thanksgiving, deepens trust, and brings restoration. I am uplifted when He welcomes me to His house and Table, takes away my sin, assures me of His guidance, strength, and paradise. The Lord is our loving Shepherd. He protects, provides, and forgives *for His own name's sake*, in keeping with His deep covenant love promised for centuries and fulfilled at Calvary. He restores and refreshes, replacing anxiousness with carefreeness, similar in a simple way as my son-in-law or daughter bringing Timmy and Peter out of the tub, into the family room with soft jammies, clean, fresh, ready for hugs and prayers, with smiles of innocent carefreeness.

The hymn's poet expands on *in* from Psalm 23:3—"He leads me in paths of righteousness"—to *within*, and so we sing *within the paths of righteousness*. My question is not the nuanced difference between *in* and *within*. Rather, why doesn't David say, "He leads me *on* paths of righteousness"? You might go up or down a sidewalk, but who goes *in* one? Who walks *in* a path? *In* expresses a state, positive or negative: Bob is in debt, Erin is in pain, and Kim is in her glory. *Paths of righteousness* are not simply trails we travel along for the sake of getting from one place to another. *Paths of righteousness* are an extension of the Shepherd's loving will for His sheep. *Paths of righteousness* are His way of life for us—a state we are in because of His love for us. These paths are second nature, automatic, so much a part of us that others associate His paths with His sheep and His sheep with His paths. They are the essence of who we are "for His name's sake" (v. 3), as the paths reflect both who He is—the giver of all good things earthly and eternal—and how we live with Him in a relationship of love and trust, desiring to please Him by our worship and trust and by serving others.

Righteous paths lead us into and through any number of things. There are righteous paths of godly living, *for His own name's sake*, as He leads us to honor Him in purity, with honesty, with a generous spirit, in serving, by maximizing ability (gifts and vocations), and by guarding against harmful behavior. Walking in righteous paths of godliness never leads to regret. But some righteous paths may lead to pain. When it is so, His children trust that because the Shepherd is leading, the path is right in His eyes. We may be uncertain of the outcome or may never come to know His precise purpose, yet we can be certain that the Shepherd uses the pain Satan introduces for our good. Pain allowed by the Shepherd is within His long-range vision. He is wise. He leads. *For His own name's sake* we trust and follow. Other righteous paths echo with God's truth from Scripture preached on a Sunday or studied in quiet solitude as the Shepherd guards us from faith-weakening false teachings and builds us up with His promises. God's truth is uplifting. Is there a better sample than this psalm's opening phrase? Psalm 23 is cherished because the truth is so comforting: *The Lord is my shepherd.*

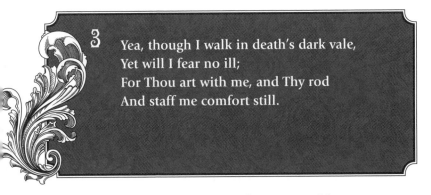

3 Yea, though I walk in death's dark vale,
Yet will I fear no ill;
For Thou art with me, and Thy rod
And staff me comfort still.

Yea, Though I Walk
in Death's Dark Vale

In this sharp contrast, we go from green pastures, beautiful waters, a restored soul, and paths of righteousness into the valley of the shadow of death. It does not last long, the good life, whether it is lavish or simple. We may be content in the Shepherd's fold, but our lives wither, and we are soon in the dark valley, as I was reminded today. The young widow whose story we told with the Baptism hymn "God's Own Child I Gladly Say It" brought to me a heartfelt note. Now a few months later, she wishes to give thanks for the benefit our congregation and community organized to support her. Steve was fifty when the Lord took him through the dark valley. Their son is in seventh grade. Their lives are not easy.

Here's another memory. A number of years ago my father-in-law, leaning against the barnyard fence post, calmly said to a friend, "And now I'll have to go through this." Having received word that his cancer was taking hold, he knew he was entering the shadows. He knew this too: *Yea, though I walk in death's dark vale, Yet will I fear no ill; For Thou art with me, and Thy rod And staff me comfort still.* Writing on the same verse from Psalm 23, Luther imagines what more David would say to expound upon his own psalm verse:

It is as if he would say: "As for me, I am indeed weak, sad, anxious, and surrounded by all kinds of danger and misfortune. Because of my sin, my heart and my conscience are not satisfied either. I experience such horrible terrors of death and hell that I almost despair. Yet though the whole world and also the gates of hell (Matthew 16:18) should oppose me, that will not dismay me. Yes, I will not be afraid of all the evil and sorrow that they may be able to lay on me; for the Lord is with me. The Lord is my counselor, comforter, protector, and helper—the Lord, I say, who has created heaven and earth and everything that is in it out of a more trifling thing than a speck of dust, that is, out of nothing. To Him all creation is subject: angels, devils, men, sin, death, etc.; in brief, He has every-thing in His power. And therefore I fear no evil."
(AE 12:168)

David fears no evil, but perhaps staring into death's face caused him to shift from talking about *what* the Shepherd does— He makes, He leads, He restores—to talking *to* the Shepherd: You are with me, You prepare, You anoint. A few nights ago—it feels embarrassing to admit—I landed in the ER. Too much walking, mowing, summer heat, and humidity, and not enough hydra-tion took me down but provided a reminder. Sooner or later, each of us enters the valley. David does not pray: *Please leadeth me* around *death's vale*. David knows that the Shepherd holds his life. David knows that the Shepherd is his way *through* death. One may wonder if Isaiah had the shepherd's song in mind, writing three centuries after David wrote Psalm 23:

But now thus says the LORD, He who created you, O Jacob, He who formed you, O Israel: "Fear not, for I have redeemed you; I have called you by name, you are Mine. When you pass through

the waters, I will be with you; and through the
rivers, they shall not overwhelm you; when you
walk through fire you shall not be burned, and the
flame shall not consume you. For I am the LORD
your God, the Holy One of Israel, your Savior. Fear
not, for I am with you." (Isaiah 43:1–3, 5)

> 4   My table Thou hast furnishèd
> In presence of my foes;
> My head Thou dost with oil anoint,
> And my cup overflows.

My Table Thou Hast Furnishèd

David feels secure and safe because the Lord of heaven and earth is his Shepherd. What do his shepherding images mean: green pastures, still waters, the shepherd's rod and staff, a furnished table in the presence of enemies, a bottomless cup, and soothing oil? The shepherd's song is a metaphor to communicate the Shepherd's care for us in life and in death. However, literally, the Lord is not a shepherd, and we are not sheep. We do not sleep and eat in green pastures. He does not literally use a rod and staff, nor does He physically walk a step ahead of us throughout the day. His hand is not massaging oil upon our heads, and while we may enjoy an abundance of food and drink, the cup is not overflowing for every Christian across the globe. As comforting as it is to know we can trust the Lord to provide, it is also true that for many of God's redeemed children, there is no rod and staff protecting from Islamic terrorism, physical abuse, domestic terror, or persecution in the mission field. For many, basic shelter, food, and water are absent. What is Psalm 23 supposed to mean for them? When it is not dehydration but a paralyzing stroke or chronic disease, a car accident or liver cancer, what soothing, healing oil and anointing are we talking about? How is Jesus, our caring Shepherd, providing and protecting in the times when it seems He is not? What does this all mean in plain English, without symbols and metaphors, without poetry?

David talked to the Lord, his Shepherd, and God welcomes us to do so too (Psalm 50:15). A shepherd, however, *calls*, and his sheep *listen*. They follow him because they know his voice. Luther urged his parishioners, and pastors today urge theirs as well, to pray to the Lord and to *listen* to what the Lord says in His Word. Certainly, all of life's good things come from God's hands, but ultimately, the deepest peace and joy come from listening to the Shepherd's voice. "I am the Good Shepherd. I know My sheep and My sheep know Me and I give them eternal life." Jesus' words are clear: "I give them eternal life" (John 10:28). Do not pay attention to what your old Adam feels; he is never satisfied. Outward appearances often deceive (1 Samuel 16:7). Let us listen to the voice of the Shepherd. Are you feeling unsatisfied? "If anyone thirsts, let him come to Me and drink" (John 7:37). Are you weary? "Come to Me, all who labor and are heavy laden, and I will give you rest" (Matthew 11:28). Is guilt weighing you down? The Lord promises, "I will remember their sins no more" (Hebrews 8:12; see also Isaiah 43:25). Typing Bible verses quickly is easy. Actually carrying a burden is not. When trials come, these are His words to live by.

People make evaluations based upon what they see. However, the world cannot see the best of what the Lord gives. He gives His best to us through what He speaks to us. You cannot *see* your sins float away, but He promises, "I forgive you." You cannot *see* His body and blood. You *see* only bread and wine, but He says, "This is My body, . . . this is My blood given and shed for you." You cannot see heaven, but He promises He is preparing a place for you. Peter reminds, "Though you have not seen Him, you love Him. Though you do not now see Him, you believe in Him" (1 Peter 1:8), and Jesus told Thomas, "Blessed are those who have not seen and yet have believed" (John 20:29).

Life situations change, feelings certainly do, and unless we are listening to Him, it is easy to lose faith, to lose the comfort that is ours in our Good Shepherd. The Lord's promise to Joshua is His promise to us: "It is the LORD who goes before you. He will be with you; He will not leave you or forsake you. Do not fear or be dismayed" (Deuteronomy 31:8). We needn't be surprised when trouble comes. "In the world you will have tribulation. But take heart; I have overcome the world" (John 16:33). David proclaims:

> For He knows our frame; He remembers that we are dust. As for man, his days are like grass; he flourishes like a flower of the field; for the wind passes over it, and it is gone, and its place knows it no more. But the steadfast love of the LORD is from everlasting to everlasting on those who fear Him, and His righteousness to children's children. (Psalm 103:14–17)

Luther's most famous hymn, "A Mighty Fortress Is Our God," refers to the devils and their desire to devour us (st. 3). One translation of stanza 4 reads: "And take they our life, Goods, fame, child, and wife, Though these all be gone, Our vict'ry has been won" (LW 289) That is correct. Even when it appears as though the Lord is not providing, not protecting, when it appears as though everything is gone, the devils have won nothing. Why? Because "The Kingdom ours remaineth." Indeed, returning to Psalm 23, *my cup overflows.*

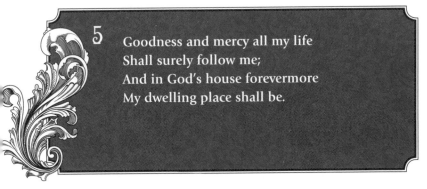

5
Goodness and mercy all my life
Shall surely follow me;
And in God's house forevermore
My dwelling place shall be.

Goodness and Mercy All My Life

Having looked at stanza 4 in the previous devotion, let us look now at the hymn's fourth and fifth stanzas together. Consider how all-encompassing is our Lord's grace.

My table Thou hast furnishèd
In presence of my foes;
My head Thou dost with oil anoint,
And my cup overflows.

Goodness and mercy all my life
Shall surely follow me;
And in God's house forevermore
My dwelling place shall be.

David announces two blessings in each of the first two lines; in the last two, he joyfully expresses the incomprehensible outcome of God's goodness and mercy. The almighty Lord is so gracious. He welcomes you and me to paradise, where He gives complete relief, peace, joy, and fulfillment—and the undeserved privilege is fully personal.

The everlasting privilege includes a strange coupling: *My table Thou hast furnishèd In presence of my foes.* How can one enjoy a meal surrounded by enemies? David is describing himself as a king who lives under the protection and blessing of the Shepherd-King, the Lord God, who has received him and is guarding him from his enemies. David sees himself as a welcome guest participating in the heavenly feast that is without end.

The shepherd imagery is beautifully comforting because David tells us the Shepherd's name. How would we pray to Jesus, talk about Jesus, trust, look forward to seeing, depend upon, thank, and praise Jesus without knowing or using His name? Using Jesus' name helps make Him real in our minds and helps exemplify what is true. We do not trust some unknown, unnamed man from long ago. God's Son was given a name (Matthew 1:21). Jesus is real, personal, and historical, an actual man who is God, who had compassion on many, died, rose, ascended, and will return. David calls God by name. He does not have a mythological god. He does not trust an imaginary deity. It is not actually a shepherd who feeds, protects, and saves us. It is *Yahweh.* In his psalms and in the accounts of his life recorded in 1 and 2 Samuel, David repeatedly addresses God by His name, *Yahweh,* printed as "Lord" in our Bibles. David knows what *Yahweh* can and would do for him, based on his experience and upon Yahweh's words of promise to him.

David is familiar with the presence of foes and threats against his life; think of the day he reached for five stones to face the nine-foot Philistine. David was not about to battle the warrior without *Yahweh's* Word and presence. In the quote below, each time you see "the Lord," read in its place *Yahweh,* the name David spoke in Hebrew, the name God first spoke of Himself to Moses (Exodus 3:14).

> And David said, "The Lord who delivered me from
> the paw of the lion and from the paw of the bear
> will deliver me from the hand of this Philistine."
> And Saul said to David, "Go, and the Lord be with
> you!" . . . Then David said to the Philistine, "You
> come to me with a sword and with a spear and
> with a javelin, but I come to you in the name of
> the Lord of hosts, the God of the armies of Israel,
> whom you have defied. This day the Lord will de-
> liver you into my hand. . . . That all this assembly

may know that the LORD saves not with sword and spear. For the battle is the LORD's, and He will give you into our hand." (1 Samuel 17:37, 45–47)

Today's foes—fear, lust, greed, guilt, regret, separation, depression, dementia, diabetes, anxieties, emphysema, and the like—are always present. When they steal, disrupt, and kill, the Lord uses our woes to increase our desire to hear His Word and to pray with David: "One thing have I asked of the LORD, that will I seek after: that I may dwell in the house of the LORD all the days of my life, to gaze upon the beauty of the LORD" (Psalm 27:4). That day will come. In Psalm 23, David writes a beautiful prayer about our Shepherd and His care for His sheep. He wants us to know precisely who this Shepherd is. He names Him twice in this psalm, framing all the promises. In the Hebrew text, *Yahweh* is the first word. *Yahweh* is my Shepherd. At the end of the psalm, there is His name again, where there will be no foes, no Goliaths, no sins, aches, threats, and anxieties in the place where we will dwell, in the house of *Yahweh* forever.

We Praise You and Acknowledge You, O God

1 We praise You and acknowledge You, O God,
    to be the Lord,
The Father everlasting, by all the
    earth adored.
To You all angel powers cry aloud, the
    heavens sing,
The cherubim and seraphim their praises
    to You bring:
"O holy, holy, holy Lord God of Sabaoth;
Your majesty and glory fill the heavens and the
earth!"

2   The band of the apostles in glory sing
        Your praise;
    The fellowship of prophets their deathless
        voices raise.
    The martyrs of Your kingdom, a great
        and noble throng,
    Sing with the holy Church throughout all
        the world this song:
    "O all-majestic Father, Your true and only Son,
    And Holy Spirit, Comforter—forever Three in
    One!"

3   You, Christ, are King of glory, the
        everlasting Son,
    Yet You, with boundless love, sought to
        rescue ev'ryone:
    You laid aside Your glory, were born of
        virgin's womb,
    Were crucified for us and were placed
        into a tomb;
    Then by Your resurrection You won for
        us reprieve—
    You opened heaven's kingdom to all who would
    believe.

4 You sit in splendid glory, enthroned at
    God's right hand,
Upholding earth and heaven by forces
    You command.
We know that You will come as our Judge
    that final day,
So help Your servants You have redeemed
    by blood, we pray;
May we with saints be numbered where
    praises never end,
In glory everlasting. Amen, O Lord, amen!

LSB 941
TEXT: STEPHEN P. STARKE, B. 1955;
COPYRIGHT © 1999 STEPHEN P. STARKE; ADMIN. CPH

hy has this hymn, in Latin called the *Te Deum*, remained prominent and deeply appreciated by the Christian Church for 1,500 years? Before proceeding to that question, there is an interesting and significant point to be made regarding the opening line. At first passing, we assume *We praise You and acknowledge You, O God, to be the Lord* means we praise You, *Father*, to be the Lord. *The Father* is cited at the start of the second line and is the object of praise in the first two stanzas. However, in the Early Christian Church, other hymns began by acknowledging *Jesus* as God. Possibly, because the apostles and early Christians gave their lives in martyrdom for confessing "Jesus is Lord" or "Jesus is God," the early hymns began with the same confession, which was so costly to many. Further, a good translation of the Latin original *Te Deum laudamus* is *We praise You as God*, rather than *We praise You, O God*. It is likely that the *Te Deum's* first line was an introductory confession that Jesus, who is human, is God (*Lutheran Service Book: Companion to the Hymns*, hymn 939). Drawn by the Spirit, we are bold to sing, to confess it is so (1 Corinthians 12:3), even as we are reminded of those in centuries past who confessed the same with their lives and who do so in oppressed nations today.

And now to this introduction's opening question—perhaps two things are responsible for the awe and appreciation Christians still hold for the *Te Deum*, the ancient text handed down to us from approximately AD 500. First, the hymn places attention and total focus upon almighty God. What is the difference between "We praise You, God" and "You, God, we praise"? The latter emphasizes *You*, the one who is being praised, not *we*, the ones doing the praising. The latter is a literal translation of the Latin *Te Deum laudamus*: "You, God, we praise," or, as noted above: "You, we praise as God." The pronoun *te* or "You" is the first word in multiple lines in the original Latin. The hymn focuses repeatedly and emphatically upon God the Father in His glorious, eternal majesty in stanzas 1 and 2, and in stanzas 3 and 4, upon the Son for having left the glory of heaven to consume all of our sin in His sacrificial suffering and death. The word order with the pronoun positioned first—*You, God, we praise*—places emphasis where it belongs and also prepares us for the hymn's delineation of why it is a blessing to us to praise Him.

Second, the hymn is treasured because it deeply enriches faith. By taking us into the world unseen, where cherubim and seraphim and saints are praising God, and by proclaiming also the reaches of Jesus Christ from glory above to the manger and cross below, the hymn uncovers the infinite expanse that distinguishes human creatures from the almighty Creator. The hymn enriches faith this way:

Stanza 1 enriches faith by

- transporting us to the invisible world of the throne room of God, known to us through the visions of Ezekiel, Isaiah, and John;

- acknowledging the complete host of angels and two types of winged creatures;

- introducing the angel's *Te Deum*, their song of praise to God, and signifying the time span throughout which they sing.

Stanza 2 enriches faith by

- marking next to God the living presence of the apostles, prophets, martyrs, and saints who join in the *Te Deum*.

Stanza 3 enriches faith by

- capturing the striking movement of the everlasting Son of God between the extreme outer boundaries of existence known to us—from the majesty and glory above, from where He departed, to the shame of the cross and tomb of death below—to where He burst forth with triumph in the power of the resurrection for the sake of all believers.

Stanza 4 enriches faith by

- imaging the Lord post ascension, seated at the highest place, at the right hand of God, from where He upholds, uses, and controls all the forces of earth and heaven;

- calling forth the truthful warning that strikes fear in any conscious mortal—that is, the One enthroned before His apostles, prophets, martyrs, saints, and angels is our Judge, and He will judge us all on the final day;

- assuring us that He redeemed us by His blood and will lift us up to be numbered with the saints, where praises never end.

COMMENTS REGARDING THE TUNE

This hymn is a terrific example of the Church borrowing something from the world to use for the Gospel's proclamation. The melody for this hymn, majestic and powerful, is from the middle of one movement of an English composer's early-twentieth-century symphony. Our author paired the melody with a translation of the *Te Deum*, which he wrote in verse form as a hymn. The melody is not overly complex, however, it would be helpful to approach it a phrase at a time or a stanza a week or to listen to the melody several times prior to singing, perhaps as preservice music, during the offering, or as a postlude. Without question, the words of the *Te Deum* call for a tune that expresses depth, strength, and joy. It has been selected as a confirmation hymn, a wedding processional, and a wedding hymn. At conferences, at our college campuses, and in some of our congregations, it is heard with trumpets, timpani, and additional instruments.

We are thankful for the writing of this hymn, the accompanying tune, and its inclusion in *Lutheran Service Book*. The music for this hymn wonderfully assists in carrying our hearts and eyes of faith to that place where the *Te Deum* is sung without ceasing.

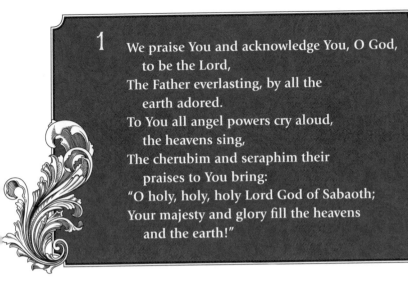

1
We praise You and acknowledge You, O God,
   to be the Lord,
The Father everlasting, by all the
   earth adored.
To You all angel powers cry aloud,
   the heavens sing,
The cherubim and seraphim their
   praises to You bring:
"O holy, holy, holy Lord God of Sabaoth;
Your majesty and glory fill the heavens
   and the earth!"

To You All Angel Powers Cry Aloud

The otherworldliness of cherubim and seraphim impresses upon us the unbounded difference between us and God, between little, mortal, severely limited, sinful children of Adam and the almighty Creator of heaven and earth, "who for us men and for our salvation come down from heaven" (Nicene Creed). Otherworldly? Consider Ezekiel's vision (1:4–28): He sees four living creatures of human likeness, each with four faces, four wings, and human hands. Each had the face of a human, a lion, an ox, and an eagle. Their appearance was like burning coals of fire and torches moving back and forth. There was for each creature a wheel-like gleaming beryl, with tall rims full of eyes all around. The creatures and wheels moved together, and their wings made the sound of the Almighty, like an army. Over their heads was a shining expanse, like brilliant crystal, and above the expanse over their heads was a throne-like sapphire, and seated was a likeness with a human appearance with gleaming metal about His waist, like the appearance of fire enclosed all around.

It is impossible to realistically imagine what Ezekiel saw and experienced when the preincarnate Son of God came to him carried by four four-winged, four-faced blazing creatures (1:4–28). We can pray, asking God to help us appreciate his response.

> Such was the appearance of the likeness of the glory of the LORD. And when I saw it, I fell on my face. (1:28)

Thinking about Ezekiel's vision of heavenly creatures exposes the canyon of power, holiness, and glory that separates us from God. It increases our sense of need for His mercy and expands our fear, love, and trust in Him.

Spending time with Dr. Hummel (*Ezekiel 1–20*, 60) brought a number of things to light. John reports that the angels never cease to say, "Holy, holy, holy, is the Lord God Almighty" (Revelation 4:8). But when did the singing begin? The answer is found in the *Te Deum* in the Order of Matins (*LSB*, p. 223): *To You cherubim and seraphim continually do cry.* The chorus has been ongoing since at least the time Isaiah heard the seraphim singing (Isaiah 6:1–3), approximately eight hundred years prior to John's revelation, and it continues now. The thought of special winged creatures singing for centuries and without end puts into perspective life's pressures.

Here's the point. To introduce the *Holy, holy, holy*, the Sanctus, in our liturgy for the Lord's Supper by saying *with angels and archangels and all the company of heaven we laud and magnify*, if I may, is like saying, "Yes, Albert Einstein and his friends and I meet for coffee to discuss physics." *What* could I possibly bring to the table, other than the coffee? And so on Sunday mornings, we enter a sacred space, the sanctuary. Can our praise—our devotion, love, and understanding—possibly match that of the powerful, holy, winged creatures of heaven? May I suggest an entrance prayer?

> O Lord, sew into my heart the posture You worked in Ezekiel's. Lead me to bow down to You with humbleness and repentance, and in the hearing and receiving of Your Word and Supper, "restore to me the joy of Your salvation" (Psalm 51:12).

Dr. Louis Brighton (*Revelation*, 128–29) taught me to think of the "holy, holy, holy," the Sanctus, as the opening refrain of the hymn sung by all the company of heaven and to recognize throughout John's Revelation a number of choral sessions whereby a variety of stanzas are added. The twenty-four elders fall down to praise Him, "for You created all things, and by Your will they existed and were created" (Revelation 4:11). John heard "every creature in heaven and on earth and under the earth and in the sea" sing their familiar verse (5:13). The people from every nation and language cry out, "Salvation belongs to our God who sits on the throne, and to the Lamb!" (7:10). All the angels of heaven sing (7:11–12), and God's people on earth in warfare add, "Just and true are Your ways. . . . Who will not fear, O Lord, and glorify Your name?" (15:3–4).

The heavenly *Te Deum*, the great hymn of praise and joy and testimony of all the angelic host, of the entire company of heaven, concludes with a magnificent "Hallelujah! Praise the Lord, our almighty God," as the multitude of saints and angels sing of God's salvation and glory and of His eternal judgment enacted against Satan, thereby securing our peace and joy—forever and ever. Hallelujah! Hallelujah!

> 2 The band of the apostles in glory sing
>   Your praise;
>   The fellowship of prophets their deathless
>   voices raise.
>   The martyrs of Your kingdom, a great
>   and noble throng,
>   Sing with the holy Church throughout
>   all the world this song:
>   "O all-majestic Father, Your true and
>   only Son,
>   And Holy Spirit, Comforter—forever
>   Three in One!"

Sing with the Holy Church throughout All the World

Each day, thousands of people visit the domed rotunda of the United States Capitol in Washington, DC, to see notable Americans commemorated in Statuary Hall. In Scripture's last book, the Holy Spirit takes John to see God seated on the throne in heaven (Revelation 4:1–3). Here live the patriarchs and apostles, dressed in white garments with golden crowns (4:4). Also there, John sees four creatures with six wings, full of eyes (4:6–8). Later, John sees a great multitude that no one could number standing before the throne and before the Lamb (7:9). He hears them cry in a loud voice, "Salvation belongs to our God who sits on the throne, and to the Lamb!" (7:10).

With this second stanza, we preview the day when John's vision becomes our reality. We will see *the band of the apostles,* including Andrew, a fisherman, whom John the Baptist led to Jesus (John 1:35–40). It was Andrew who told Jesus about the boy with five loaves and two fish (6:8–9). And he was one of the four who asked Jesus about Judgment Day (Mark 13:3–4). Without Andrew's evangelism efforts, perhaps we wouldn't meet Peter (John 1:42). And Andrew's comment about the boy's fish and bread leads to the Lord's display of raw power, which He uses to steady His apostles' faith (John 6:1–14; Luke 9:10–17). Andrew continued to tell others the Good News he received in Christ until, according to tradition, he was crucified for doing so.

THE MARTYRS OF YOUR KINGDOM, A GREAT AND NOBLE THRONG

John also saw this graphic illustration of satanic evil: "the woman, drunk with the blood of the saints, the blood of the martyrs of Jesus" (Revelation 17:6). God takes death seriously; He will punish those who murder His people. Read Revelation 16:4–6. Viola Fronkova, our Slovakian friend, told me about Pastor Uhorskai. The Communist secret police imprisoned him on March 14, 1951. Accused of having loaned two anti-Marxist books to students, Pastor Uhorskai was fined, interrogated, and beaten repeatedly. All of his property was confiscated. For thirty-nine more years, he was not allowed to serve his parish. In 1990, the Slovak Lutheran Church elected him as bishop. He said, "You ask how I dealt with the loss of a normal life. . . . I knew . . . it is a narrow path with the Lord Jesus! During interrogations, I recall a time they were furious because they could not break my spirit. I was lying down, beaten, unable to move my hands or legs, unable to speak, but was convinced of Christ's presence with me. We can go through suffering with this expectation: The Lord has His schedule; He knows when to rescue us" (email from Viola Fronkova, December 6, 2018).

Pastor Uhorskai did not die a martyr's death, though I believe he gladly would have. Christian martyrs express unmatched commitment born of God's gift of faith. Few if any of us will be called to honor our Lord through martyrdom. However, we can strive first to love God and serve neighbor, also hoping for the additional result that others would be encouraged to trust the Lord always and to stand up for Him regardless the cost. For example, if I may speak to mothers and fathers of little children, imagine overhearing, "Dear Jesus, thank You for my mom and dad. Thank You for their love. Thank You for making them so strong in faith that they would die for You. I know they would. Make my faith strong like theirs. Amen." Other suggestions: Lead your families and friends to the Lord's house to hear His Word. Sing an unashamed, joyful noise unto the Lord. Talk with your children and friends about the apostles, prophets, and martyrs. Be a guide for others past distractions that threaten faith. Stand for what matters. Be like Andrew—tell someone, "Death is coming, but hell is worse. Jesus suffered hell for you and defeated death too. May I tell you more?" Pray, "Dear Jesus, use me by what I say and do to draw others closer to You. Thank You for making me Your child in Baptism. Thank You for forgiving me. Guard my faith and keep me close by Your side for Jesus' sake. Amen."

As the Lord uses others to encourage us in the faith, we pray that others will be built up through us too. The Lord uses the martyrs and the faith He worked in them to strengthen ours. John knew that the martyrs were saved by the Lamb's blood, not their own blood—by the hearing of the Good News—and he said of them that "they loved not their lives even unto death" (Revelation 12:11). The Holy Spirit will use John's vision in Revelation to grant to us such faith until the day when, by His grace, He gathers us to sing with the apostles, prophets, martyrs, and the Holy Church through time:

> O all-majestic Father, Your true and only Son,
>
> And Holy Spirit, Comforter—forever Three in One!

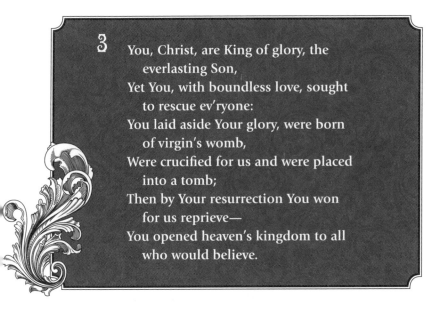

3 You, Christ, are King of glory, the
       everlasting Son,
   Yet You, with boundless love, sought
       to rescue ev'ryone:
   You laid aside Your glory, were born
       of virgin's womb,
   Were crucified for us and were placed
       into a tomb;
   Then by Your resurrection You won
       for us reprieve—
   You opened heaven's kingdom to all
       who would believe.

You, Christ, Are King of Glory

The glory that surrounds God is incomprehensible to us. The *Te Deum* shifts focus from the praise given to Him (sts. 1–2) to the reason all praise belongs to Him. *You, Christ, are King of glory, the everlasting Son. . . . You, with boundless love, sought to rescue ev'ryone.* He could accomplish the rescue only if He would exchange His seat in heaven for every sinner's place in hell. Praise belongs to God because Jesus left glory to take judgment. In the introduction of this hymn, we said that the *Te Deum* fills our hearts with joy and confidence in Christ by proclaiming our Lord's journey from His eternal majesty in the heavenly throne room to the scorching shame and degradation of His suffering, crucifixion, and death.

As Americans earn more, they typically spend more. True, some enjoy saving more than they enjoy spending. But few of us understand sacrificing, defined here as giving up the pleasures and comforts we have learned to enjoy. A couple may give a $10,000 or $12,000 offering from a $100,000 income, and that is not unfaithful, but neither is it really sacrificial. Or a person may help their neighbor for a couple hours, but there remains ample time for relaxation. We will and sometimes do sacrifice for others, but we rather dimly comprehend it compared to the One "who, though He was . . . God, . . . emptied Himself. . . . He humbled himself . . . to the point of death" (Philippians 2:6–8). First, He was there with the Father and the Spirit—eternally— before God created everything out of nothing. In the beginning, He was not doing physical tasks. Rather, He was doing things only God could do—creating, overseeing, and sustaining everything He had made (John 1:1, 3; Colossians 1:15–16; Hebrews 1:1–3). His was no position of weakness. How much power belongs to the One who sustains natural laws, like gravity, so acorns fall and so the sun holds the earth in orbit to mark each year and to keep us from freezing!

Prior to His incarnation, the Son was willingly serving and protecting His people of Old Testament times. The Son of God, preincarnate, is "the angel of the LORD" who speaks to Abraham and who provides the ram to prevent him from sacrificing his only son (Genesis 22:9–14). He speaks to Moses from inside the burning bush (Exodus 3:4–6). He is "the commander of the LORD's army" who appears to Joshua before the battles begin (Joshua 5:13–15). And He likely is the fourth man who appears in the fiery furnace to rescue the three men of God (Daniel 3:24–25).

God the Father, the Son preincarnate, and the Holy Spirit continually intervened, interrupting history, for the well-being of God's children, ultimately to guide things in keeping with the covenant promise to Abraham to *rescue ev'ryone* through his offspring (Genesis 12:1–3).

Now the time had come for the Son to sacrifice. He could no longer stay preincarnate. Laying aside heaven's glory is no trivial thing. The virgin birth is miraculous, and the manger speaks of humility, but what He came to do is another thing entirely. It is shocking—we know that God the Son creates, loves, forgives, heals, helps, protects, serves, feeds, and more. However, none of those is the verb used in the Apostles' Creed. What is that verb? He "suffered." He did not leave the glory of heaven for more spectacular surroundings. He was conceived to suffer unparalleled misery and pain. Crucifixion is vicious and disgustingly barbaric. Others suffered as He did and were also whipped, scourged, and nailed up to die. What made His worse? It is not the treatment He received from His earthly enemies. Rather, what made it worse was the treatment He received from His heavenly Father—all the wrath of God for all sin for all time (Isaiah 53:10; Hebrews 2:9; 10:10; 1 John 2:2). For all sin—yours and mine. In order to destroy the sinful disease slithering within us, Jesus suffered hell. Hell is a lake that burns with fire and sulfur (Revelation 21:8). Hell is eternal destruction, away from the presence of the Lord and from the glory of His might (2 Thessalonians 1:9). It is where the damned will drink the wine of God's wrath, poured full strength into the cup of His anger (Revelation 14:10). And hell is where the condemned have no rest, day or night, and the smoke of their torment goes up forever (Revelation 14:11). Jesus suffered hell—all of it—for you, for me.

And that is why the *King of glory is worthy of all praise.* How unmatched is His love. How fitting is the adjective we sing to describe it: *Yet You, with* boundless *love, sought to rescue ev'ryone.*

4 You sit in splendid glory, enthroned at
    God's right hand,
  Upholding earth and heaven by forces
    You command.
  We know that You will come as our
    Judge that final day,
  So help Your servants You have
    redeemed by blood, we pray;
  May we with saints be numbered
    where praises never end,
  In glory everlasting. Amen,
    O Lord, amen!

You Sit in Splendid Glory

On the island of Patmos, in a time of worship, John is commissioned by a loud, trumpetlike voice to write and to send to the churches what he sees (Revelation 1:9–11). John is given to see a stunning vision of one like the Son of Man, dressed in a flowing robe with a golden sash, His hair white as wool, His eyes like flames of fire, feet like burnished brass fired in a furnace. His voice roars like rushing waters. He holds seven stars, a sharp, two-edged sword protrudes from His mouth, and His whole appearance is like the sun in full power. These dramatic aspects of the Lord's appearance are linked to honor, wisdom, and glory (Proverbs 16:31; 20:29), to the purifying presence of God (Malachi 3:2), to the power to destroy evil (Daniel 2:33), to the authority over angels (Matthew 25:31), to executing justice (Isaiah 11:4; Hebrews 4:12), and are a sign that He radiates the glory and grace-bestowing light of God (Malachi 4:2; Hebrews 1:3). All of this and more John reports in five verses (Revelation 1:12–16), and he is struck down by the sight of it, as if by the force of death (1:17). The entire vision goes on for twenty-two chapters.

The trumpetlike voice calls John through an open door to heaven, and the vision changes (Revelation 4:1). John sees *Yahweh* seated on the throne. He sees the twenty-four elders seated around Him. He sees and hears the six-winged creatures sing the continual chorus, the refrain of the *Te Deum* (4:1–8), together with all the saints acclaiming Him to be worthy of glory, honor, and power. Why? They know! "You created all things, and by Your will they existed and were created" (4:11). John sees and hears angels and saints singing. It is unimaginable!

We confess in our creeds every Sunday that God is worthy of all praise for His creation. Yes, our Father deserves all praise for His creation, and John witnesses the most magnificent chorus of praise by angels, heavenly creatures, and all the saints offered to the Creator, who is seated on the throne. However, John does not see Jesus. Where is He? John sees a sealed scroll in God's right hand. An angel cries out for anyone worthy to open the scroll. No one steps forth. Who can stand before the Lord (1 Samuel 6:20; Psalms 76:7; 130:3)? There is not one worthy creature in heaven or on earth (Revelation 5:1–4). John weeps! The implication is that if no one is worthy to open the scroll, the eternal destiny, the salvation of all is in jeopardy. If no one is worthy to open the scroll, the heavenly chairs for God's children will remain empty forever.

"Weep no more!" an elder declares to John (Revelation 5:5). Standing between the throne and the four living creatures, John sees the Lamb as though it had been slain (v. 6). Earlier, Jesus is introduced as the Son of Man, who strikes fear, but here He is introduced as the Lamb. For God's people standing before the Lamb, there is no fear. He is "our Passover lamb, [who] has been sacrificed" (1 Corinthians 5:7). He is the Lamb who came to take away the sin of the world (John 1:29), the Lamb who would die for us while we were still sinning (Romans 5:8), who was pierced for our transgressions (Isaiah 53:5), who redeemed us from the eternal curse of the Law, having become a curse for us (Galatians 3:13). He is the Lamb who is the propitiation for our sins (1 John 2:2), whose precious blood, not silver and gold, has ransomed us (1 Peter 1:18–19).

He is the Lamb who is received by His Father simultaneously as His disciples see Him ascend on the clouds (Acts 1:9–10). The disciples see Him going up; John sees Him coming in. John sees the enthronement and crowning of the Lamb who alone is worthy—by virtue of His holy life, crucifixion, death, and resurrection—to receive the scroll. The scroll marks the giving to the Lamb the complete, uninterrupted lordship of heaven and earth, the full reigning power over all dominions, authorities, events, ideologies, wars, outcomes, governments, and ambitions of people. And even more, the absolute control of the judgment of the whole human race is given to "the Lamb who was slain." Praise God! (See Brighton, 134–140; 144–145)

When the Son ascended, when He returned to His heavenly Father, there began a celebration unlike any other. It has been ongoing for two thousand years. It has only begun. It will never end. The perfect Son, who came to earth to suffer for wayward sons and daughters, returns to glory victorious and is welcomed with everlasting praise. John weeps no more. He sees the Lamb take the scroll from the right hand of God. He sees the six-winged creatures and the twenty-four elders fall down before the Lamb. They sing a new song (Revelation 5:7–10), and John hears around the throne and the six-winged creatures and the elders the voice of many angels numbering myriads of myriads all saying with a loud voice,

> Worthy is the Lamb who was slain, to receive
> power and wealth and wisdom and might and
> honor and glory and blessing! (5:12)

He *was* slain. He *is* risen. He *now* reigns. He *is* praised, and the day is soon coming when with "every creature in heaven and on earth and under the earth and in the sea, and all that is in them" we will be numbered, saying, "To Him who sits on the throne and to the Lamb be blessing and honor and glory and might forever and ever! . . . Amen!" (5:13–14).

Bibliography

Brighton, Louis A. *Revelation* Concordia Commentary. St. Louis: Concordia, 1999.

Chemnitz, Martin, and Johann Gerhard. *The Doctrine of Man* Concordia Heritage Series. Augsburg: Minneapolis, 1962.

Concordia Self-Study Bible. NIV. Concordia: St. Louis, 1986.

Franzmann, Martin H. *Follow Me: Discipleship according to St. Matthew.* St. Louis: Concordia, 1961.

Gibbs, Jeffrey A. *Matthew 1:1–11:1* Concordia Commentary. St. Louis: Concordia, 2006.

———. *Matthew 11:2–20:34* Concordia Commentary. St. Louis: Concordia, 2010.

———. *Matthew 21:1–28:20* Concordia Commentary. St. Louis: Concordia, 2018.

Giertz, Bo. *To Live with Christ.* St. Louis: Concordia, 2008.

Hummel, Horace D. *Ezekiel 1–20* Concordia Commentary. St. Louis: Concordia, 2005.

———. *Ezekiel 21–48* Concordia Commentary. St. Louis: Concordia, 2007.

Just, Arthur A., Jr. *Luke 1:1–9:50* Concordia Commentary. St. Louis: Concordia, 1996.

———. *Luke 9:51–24:53* Concordia Commentary. St. Louis: Concordia, 1997.

Kolb, Robert. *Luther and the Stories of God.* Grand Rapids: Baker, 2012.

Kolb, Robert, and Charles P. Arand. *The Genius of Luther's Theology.* Grand Rapids: Baker, 2008.

Lutheran Service Book: Companion to the Hymns. 2 vols. St. Louis: Concordia, 2019.

Lessing, R. Reed. *Isaiah 40–55* Concordia Commentary. St. Louis: Concordia, 2011.

Middendorf, Michael P. *Romans 1–8* Concordia Commentary. St. Louis: Concordia, 2013.

———. *Romans 9–16* Concordia Commentary. St. Louis: Concordia, 2016.

Mitchell, Christopher W. *Our Suffering Savior.* St. Louis: Concordia, 2005.

———. *Song of Songs* Concordia Commentary. St. Louis: Concordia, 2003.

Peters, Albrecht. *Baptism and the Lord's Supper.* St. Louis: Concordia, 2012.

Rutledge, Fleming. *The Crucifixion.* Grand Rapids: Eerdmans, 2017.

Sasse, Hermann. *We Confess the Sacraments.* Vol. 2, *We Confess Anthology*, trans. Norman Nagel. St. Louis: Concordia, 1998.

Van Dyke, Henry. *The Story of the Psalms.* New York: Charles Scribner's Sons, 1910.

Vajda, Jaroslav J. *Now the Joyful Celebration.* St. Louis: Morning Star, 1987.

Voelz, James W. *Mark 1:1–8:26* Concordia Commentary. St. Louis: Concordia, 2013.

Weinrich, William C. *John 1:1–7:1* Concordia Commentary. St. Louis: Concordia, 2015.

Winger, Thomas M. *Ephesians* Concordia Commentary. St. Louis: Concordia, 2015.

Wright, N. T. *The Resurrection of the Son of God.* Minneapolis: Fortress Press, 2003.

Scripture Index